To Mike
From Mark & Carol
82 DEC 25

NAVAL ARMAMENT

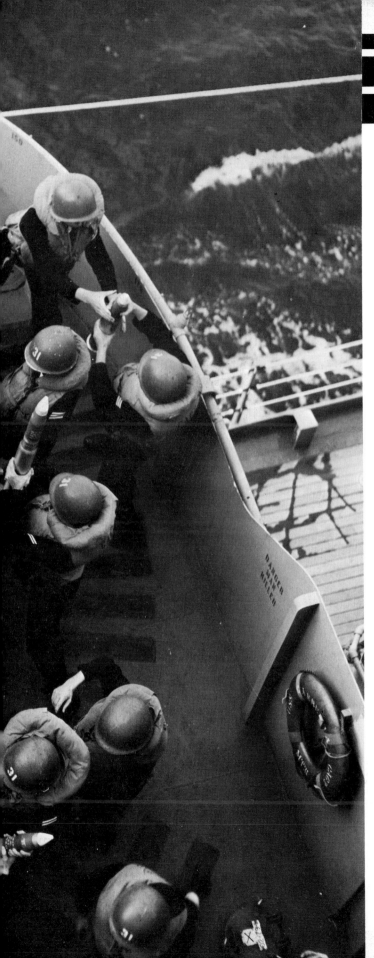

Doug Richardson

NAVAL
ARMAMENT

JANE'S

LONDON · NEW YORK · SYDNEY

First published in the United Kingdom in 1981 by
Jane's Publishing Company Limited
238 City Road, London EC1V 2PU

ISBN 0 7106 0127 1

Published in the United States of America in 1982 by
Jane's Publishing Incorporated
730 Fifth Avenue
New York
N.Y. 10019

ISBN 0 531 03738 X

Picture research by J. G. Moore

Computer Typesetting by Method Limited
Woodford Green, Essex

Printed in Great Britain by Biddles Limited,
Guildford, Surrey

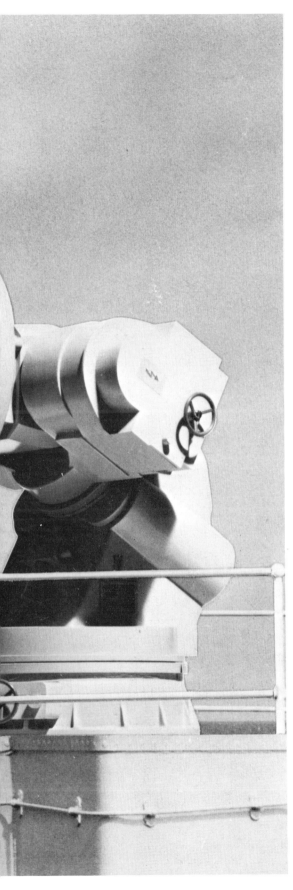

CONTENTS

ACKNOWLEDGEMENTS

Page 8, Aérospatiale; 9 Lockheed, MoD; 10, Lockheed; 11, General Dynamics; 12, US Navy; 15, Tass, Novosti; 17, Aérospatiale; 19, Aérospatiale; 21, Israel Aircraft Industries; 23, Kongsberg Vapenfabrikk; 24, Saab-Scania; 25, US Navy; 26, General Dynamics; 29, Novosti; 30, Novosti; 32, MoD; 37, Thomson-CSF; 39, Selenia; 40, Shorts; 41, MoD; 43, MoD; 45, RCA; 46, US Navy; 49, Ford Aerospace, US Navy; 50, General Dynamics; 51, Bendix; 52, US Navy; 53, General Dynamics; 54, Tass, Novosti; 55, US Navy; 58, Canadian Armed Forces; 60, ECP Armées; 61, Marine Nationale; 62, ECP Armées; 64, Rheinmetall; 69, Breda; 70, Breda; 76, Bofors; 77, Royal Netherlands Navy; 78, Bofors; 79, Bofors; 80, Karlskronavaret; 82, Bofors; 84, Oerlikon-Bührle; 85, Oerlikon-Bührle; 86, MoD; 87, MoD; 88, MoD; 89, Chilean Navy; 92, US Navy; 95, US Navy, Chilean Navy; 97, US Navy; 98, US Navy; 99, US Navy; 101, Swiftships Inc.; 102, Emerson Electric; 104, US Navy; 105, MoD; 107, MoD; 108, MoD; 109, MoD; 110, US Navy; 111, Novosti, John Moore; 112, John Moore; 115, AEG-Telefunken; 117, Whitehead Moto Fides; 118, FFV; 119, FFV, MoD; 121, Marconi, MoD; 125, US Navy; 126, Northrop; 128, British Aerospace, Latécoère; 129, Kongsberg Vapenfabrikk; 130, Bofors; 131, US Navy; 132, US Navy; 133, Goodyear Aerospace; 135, Tass; 136, MoD; 139, C & S Taylor, IWM; 141, IWM.

All pictures except pp 28, 36, 44, 47, 55, 83, 84, 91, 94, 100, 105, 106 and 111 via MARS, London.

In preparing this book, based largely on the late Denis Archer's *Jane's Pocket Book of Naval Armament*, I have left the basic form of the book unaltered, providing the reader with a convenient source of information on most of the surface and submarine weapons currently or imminently in naval service. The only significant change is the modified layout of the sections dealing with Naval Ordnance and Torpedoes which have been brought into line with the scheme adopted in *Jane's Weapon Systems*. Instead of being listed in order of calibre, naval guns are now divided up according to their nation of origin, so that all guns produced by a single nation are grouped together in descending order of calibre. Torpedoes are grouped according to nation of origin, and are then listed alphabetically by designation.

Most of the updating task consisted of adding new entries, deletions being largely confined to the weeding out of programmes which never came to fruition and eliminating guns carried by US Second World War vintage cruisers which have finally been scrapped. The Soviet Navy accounts for what many must see as more than its fair share of new weapons — three new SLBMs, three new anti-ship missiles, three new surface-to-air missiles and four new anti-submarine missiles. Over the same period of time, the United States has been responsible for six new entries, three of which are naval guns of 76 mm calibre or less.

The only category of naval weapon not covered is that of mines. The amount of data on this subject has increased significantly since the first edition was published but is still not sufficient to allow a comprehensive treatment.

For purely nostalgic reasons it is good to see one link with the past preserved in this edition — the entry for the US Navy 16-inch gun carried by the *Iowa* class battleships. If the new US Administration proceeds with its plans to bring one or more of these vessels out of retirement, these relics of a long-gone era may feature in a future third edition of "Naval Armament" as a link to the days before the strike aircraft, guided missile and nuclear warhead made traditional battlefleets a thing of the past.

STRATEGIC MISSILES

CSS-N-X MISSILE

China is known to be developing a submarine-launched ballistic missile similar in configuration and performance to the US Polaris weapon. One report claims that deployment aboard the first of six modified *Han* class submarines is likely in 1981, but the US Department of Defense report for Fiscal Year 1981 states simply that "There is no progress to report on the SLBM program of the PRC, although work probably continues on a nuclear-powered submarine and a solid-fuel missile to go with it."

MSBS BALLISTIC MISSILES

France continues with dogged determination to develop and expand its SLBM fleet. Five submarines are now operational, all carrying the M-20 missile which has replaced the earlier M-1 and M-2.

When the first two submarines entered service in the early 1970s they were armed with the 2,500-km (1,350-nm) range M-1, while the next two carried the 3,400-km (1,840-nm) range M-2. The present-day M-20 entered service with the fifth vessel and carried penetration aids to help the warhead avoid ABM defences.

In order to obtain a further increase in range, French designers have opted to use a three-stage configuration. The resulting M-4 weapon will carry five to seven MRVs and not MIRVs as has been reported in the past. Flight trials will be conducted from the experimental submarine *Gymnote* and the weapon is due to become operational in 1985 aboard the sixth French ballistic-missile submarine *L'Inflexible*. It will then be retrofitted to the other five vessels.

Missile Data
Length: M-20 10.4 m
M-4 11.05 m
Diameter: M-20 150 cm
M-4 193 cm
Launch weight: M-20 20 tons
M-4 35 tons
Propulsion: M-20 2-stage solid propellant
M-4 3-stage solid propellant
Guidance: inertial
Warhead: M-20 nuclear, 1 MT
M-4 5-7 MRVs, 150 KT each
Range: M-20 3,400 km (1,825 nm)
M-4 4,500 km (2,430 nm)
Date introduced: M-1 1971
M-2 1975
M-20 1977

Manufacturer
Missile system contractor: Aérospatiale

Status
Operational aboard five French Navy *Le Redoutable* class submarines.

Below: First generation MSBS M-1 missile. *Right:* Launch of an MSBS M-20 ballistic missile from a submerged French Navy submarine.

(USA)

As the new Trident-armed *Ohio* class ballistic-missile submarines enter service, the US Navy intends to phase out the last ten Polaris-armed *George Washington* class submarines. All should be withdrawn by the end of 1981. Under current plans, eight of these vessels will be converted into attack submarines.

Several versions of Polaris were deployed by the US Navy during the weapon's 20-year career. The early single-warhead Polaris A-1 has a range of 2,220 km (1,200 nm) but was soon replaced by the 2,780-km (1,500-nm) range A-2 model. When the definitive 2,880-km (1555-nm) range A-3 entered service, it carried a single re-entry vehicle but was modified in the early 1970s to carry three 200 KT warheads.

(UK)

This pioneering SLBM will remain in Royal Navy service until the planned British fleet of Trident-armed vessels becomes operational in the early 1990s. In order to keep the system effective until then, Britain has spent about £1,000 million on a new warhead system. Known as Chevaline, it will add advanced penetration aids and the ability to manoeuvre the payload in space but will not constitute a true MIRV system. RN Polaris rounds were built in the USA as was the missile-launching equipment but both the Chevaline "front-end" and the earlier triple MRVs were of British design and manufacture.

POLARIS A-3 MISSILE

Missile Data
Length: 9.7 m
Diameter: 137 cm
Launch weight: 16 tons
Propulsion: 2-stage solid propellant
Guidance: inertial
Warhead: 3 200 KT MRVs
Range: 4,600 km (2,500 nm)
Date introduced: 1964 (with single warhead)

Manufacturer
Main system contractor: Lockheed Missiles and Space

Status
Production complete.

RN POLARIS MISSILE

Missile Data
See US Polaris entry above

Status
Operational on four *Resolution* class submarines of the Royal Navy.

Left: Polaris A-3 breaks surface. *Above:* Royal Navy Polaris.

POSEIDON C-3 MISSILE   (USA)

For many years a mainstay of the US Navy strategic missile force, the Poseidon fleet is now slowly being reduced in numbers as *Benjamin Franklin* class submarines are retrofitted with Trident missiles. At present each missile carries ten independently targetable warheads of 50 KT yield but an unconfirmed report claims that 300 existing missiles will have their warheads upgraded to 100 KT when the latter require routine replacement of life-expired chemical explosive components.

Poseidon remains operational aboard the *Lafayette* class of ballistic-missile submarine and the force strength will stabilise at 19 vessels once the Trident conversion programme is over. An undisclosed number of warheads are assigned to NATO targets.

Poseidon C-3 on its test launching pad.

Missile Data
Length: 10.4 m
Diameter: 188 cm
Launch weight: 27 tons
Propulsion: 2-stage solid propellant
Guidance: improved inertial
Warhead: MIRV with 14RV capacity currently 10 50 KT plus penaids
Range: 4,600 km (2,500 nm)
Date introduced: 1971

Manufacturer
System contractor: Lockheed Missiles and Space

Status
Operational in *Lafayette* submarines of the USN.

By combining recent advances in the fields of micro-miniaturised electronics and small turbofan engines, the US Navy has been able to order the development of a class of cruise missiles far in advance of the weapons of this type carried by Soviet warships. Intended for launching from standard USN 21-inch (53.3-cm) torpedo tubes or from fixed launchers on surface ships, Tomahawk may be used for both tactical and strategic missions.

In the strategic role, Tomahawk will carry a nuclear warhead over a range of 2,400-3,200 km (1,300-1,730 nm) but for tactical (anti-ship) missions will deliver a 454-kg high-explosive warhead at ranges of 480 km (260 nm) or more. The need to differentiate between strategic and tactical cruise missiles for the purposes of SALT negotiations has caused some of the impetus to be drained from the Tomahawk programme, and much of the current attention is being paid to the proposed land-based GLCM (Ground-Launched Cruise Missile) variant.

Operational evaluation of Tomahawk by the US Navy should be completed by mid 1982 and could lead to a production decision but there are currently no firm plans for this phase of the programme.

During the over-water portion of its flight, Tomahawk will rely on inertial navigation. Once over land, it will update its navigation system at regular intervals using terrain contour matching (TERCOM) guidance — a system which compares the terrain profile recorded by the missile's radar altimeter with pre-recorded geographical data held in its computer memory. Use of TERCOM is expected to result in miss distances measurable in tens of metres. Anti-ship rounds would fly towards the target under inertial guidance, performing a "pop-up" manoeuvre near its destination so that the missile-seeker head can acquire and lock onto the target.

Missile Data
Length: 625 cm (including booster)
Body Diameter: 53 cm
Wing span: 254 cm
Launch weight: 1,443 kg
Propulsion: solid-propellant rocket booster plus turbofan
Guidance: strategic, inertial plus TERCOM tactical, inertial plus active radar seeker
Warhead: strategic W-80 nuclear (200 KT) tactical 454-kg HE
Cruising speed: Mach 0.7
Maximum range: strategic up to 3,200 km (1,730 nm) tactical 480 km+ (260 nm+)

Manufacturer
General Dynamics

Status
Development under operational evaluation by the US Navy.

Tomahawk on test flight.

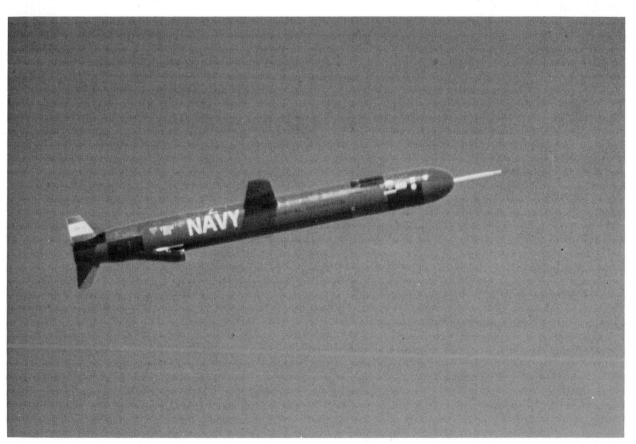

In laying down the specification for Trident, the US Navy set out to obtain a weapon with twice the range of Poseidon but with greater accuracy. The Mk 5 guidance system performs a similar function to that of the Mk 3 used in the earlier weapon but uses a stellar-inertial sensor to update the trajectory during the post-boost phase of flight. After separation from the third stage, the post-boost vehicle corrects the trajectory using data generated by the stellar update, then dispenses the individual warheads onto the appropriate flight-paths.

Trident will be deployed aboard at least three classes of submarines — the custom-built *Ohio* class, retrofitted Poseidon vessels of the *Benjamin Franklin* class and aboard a new class of Royal Navy submarines. Two fire-control systems have been announced to date. *Ohio* class vessels will be fitted with the Mk 89 Mod 0, while ex-Poseidon boats will receive the Mk 88 Mod 2. First operational deployment of the weapon was on the USS *Francis Scott Key* which sailed for its first Trident-armed patrol in October 1979. The first *Ohio* class submarine slipped badly in timescale, but was due operational in late 1981. At least seven more *Ohio*s are planned, while long lead time items have been ordered for several more. A total of 12 Poseidon boats are due for conversion to operate Trident. Britain's decision to procure Trident was announced in the summer of 1980. The fleet will probably consist of four or five vessels built in UK shipyards.

Current plans call for the development of an improved Trident II missile for deployment in the late 1980s. This weapon would have a range of up to 11,000 km (5,940 nm), carry about ten 350 KT MIRVs and have an accuracy rivalling that ot the land-based Minuteman ICBM force.

Missile Data
Length: 10.38 m
Diameter: 88 cm
Launch weight: 32 tons
Propulsion: 3-stage solid propellant
Guidance: stellar-inertial
Warhead: nuclear, 7 100 KT MIRVs
Range: 7,000 km (3,780 nm)
Date introduced: 1979

Manufacturer
System contractor: Lockheed Missiles and Space

Status
Operational aboard US Navy converted *Benjamin Franklin* class and *Ohio* class submarines.

Trident second test launch.

SOVIET SUBMARINE-LAUNCHED BALLISTIC MISSILES

There are five basic types of significant and currently operational submarine-launched ballistic missile in service with the Soviet Navy. Such brief details of these missiles as are available are given in the entries following this one; but because the place of these missiles in the general pattern of Soviet naval development is best understood by reference to the parallel submarine development programme, some brief notes on relevant submarines are appended.

Zulu-V Class
Diesel-powered submarine converted in 1955-57 for surface launch of ballistic missiles. First trials were with an adapted Scud-A missile system developed for the Red Army: subsequently the short-range missile known by the NATO code-name Sark or the US code SS-N-4 was installed. None are currently operational.

Golf Class
Diesel-powered submarine built to launch ballistic missiles from the surface. Originally equipped with the SS-N-4 (Sark), about half the class were later converted to the improved SS-N-5 (Serb) missile. Golf class submarines entered service around 1960 and the first Serb conversions became operational in about 1968. The few vessels remaining in service are probably trials ships rather than operational submarines — one Golf-III (3 × SS-N-8 missiles), one Golf-IV (3 × SS-N-6) and one Golf-V (3 × SS-NX-20).

Hotel Class
These were the first nuclear-powered Russian submarines to be equipped with ballistic missiles. Like the Golf class boats they were first equipped with Sark missiles in launch tubes mounted in the fin, and first became operational around 1960. All submarines in this class, however, were converted to carry the SS-N-5 Serb missile between 1963 and 1967; and it was only after these conversions were complete that the Golf class conversion began. Seven of these submarines are believed to be operational.

Yankee Class
Similar to the US Lafayette class, these submarines were built to carry a much-improved ballistic missile suitable for underwater launch which is positively known as the SS-N-6 and probably bears the NATO code-name Sawfly. The nuclear-powered submarine carries 16 of these missiles. Thirty-three of these submarines, which entered service around 1968, are believed to be operational. A total of 34 Hotel class was built, but not all now carry the SS-N-6. Several have had their missile tubes removed, while one was converted into a trials ship for the SS-N-17.

Delta Classes
At the beginning of the 1980s the Soviet Navy operated 32 Delta class submarines armed with SS-N-8 and SS-N-18 missiles. Fifteen are 12-round Delta I vessels but the 16-round Delta II was displaced by the SS-N-18-armed Delta III after only four had been built.

Typhoon Class
Little is known about these large vessels beyond the fact that they are expected to carry between 20 and 24 missiles. First vessel of the class was launched at Severodvinsk in September 1980 and is reported to have a displacement of 30,000 tons — more than a third greater than the US Ohio class and three times that of the Delta class.

SS-N-5 (SERB) BALLISTIC MISSILE

The most advanced of the first generation of Russian submarine-launched ballistic missiles, the SS-N-5 is still operationally deployed although it can be launched only from the surface. It is believed to be ejected from its launch tube by cold gas generators which are jettisoned when the main motor fires. By modern standards, this missile must be considered obsolescent.

Missile Data
Length: 11-13 m
Diameter: 120-150 cm
Launch weight: 13-18 tons
Propulsion: storable liquid
Guidance: inertial
Warhead: nuclear, single
Range: 1,300 km (700 nm)
Date introduced: 1963

Status
Operational in a few *Hotel* class submarines.

SS-N-6 (SAWFLY) BALLISTIC MISSILE

First of the second-generation, dived-launch, Russian SLBM, this missile is designated SS-N-6 in the US code and known as Sawfly to NATO. The weapon is no longer in production, some 1,000 rounds having been delivered.

According to US official statements three models of this missile have been observed. The first two are single-warhead weapons, Mod 2 having a greater range than Mod 1: the third has a 3-warhead MRV arrangement. According to US sources, the Mod 2 and 3 versions can reach any target in the USA from firing positions on the 100-fathom contour line off the US coast.

Missile Data
Length: 9.65 m
Diameter: 165 cm
Launch weight: 20 tons
Propulsion: storable liquid
Guidance: inertial
Warhead: Mods 1 and 2 nuclear, single
        Mod 3 3 MRVs
Range: Mod 1 2,400 km (1,300 nm)
      Mod 2 and 3 3,000 km (1,600 nm)
Date introduced: Mod 1 1968
          Mods 2 and 3 1974

Status
Currently the most widely deployed Russian SLBM. All three versions are operational although Mod 1 is expected to be phased out gradually. All are deployed on *Yankee* class submarines.

SS-N-8 BALLISTIC MISSILE

When the SS-N-8 entered service in 1973 it gave the Soviet Navy, for the first time, a ballistic missile which outranged its US counterparts. Even the 7,000-km (3,785-nm) range of Trident is eclipsed by the almost 8,000-km (4,325-nm) reach of this impressive weapon which uses stellar-inertial guidance to achieve a CEP of only 400 m. First rounds in service were the Mod 1 variant carrying a single warhead of 1-2 MT yield but a Mod 2 fitted with three MRVs has been reported.

Missile Data
Length: 12.95 m
Diameter: 165 cm
Launch weight: 28-30 tons
Propulsion: storable liquid
Guidance: stellar-inertial
Warhead: Mod 1 nuclear, single
        Mod 2 nuclear, 3 MRVs
Range: 7,800 km (4,200 nm)
Date introduced: 1973

Status
Operational in *Delta-I* and *Delta-II* class nuclear submarines of the Soviet Navy.

Serb missiles on parade.

Sawfly missiles in Red Square.

SS-NX-17 BALLISTIC MISSILE

(USSR)

Although first test-fired in 1975 and at sea since 1977, this missile remains something of an unknown factor. The first Soviet SLBM to abandon the well-tried liquid propellant, it is fitted with a post-boost vehicle of the type normally used to release MIRVs, but carries only a single warhead. The exact status of the single *Yankee* class submarine to which it has been fitted is also unknown. US reference to this missile as the SS-NX-17 suggests that it is not operationally deployed, although more accurate than the widely used SS-N-6.

Missile Data
Length: 11 m
Diameter: 165 cm
Launch weight: unknown
Propulsion: 2-stage solid propellant
Guidance: inertial
Warhead: nuclear, single
Range: 5,000 km (2,700 nm)
Date introduced: 1977

Status
Installed aboard a single *Yankee* class submarine of the Soviet Navy.

SS-N-18 BALLISTIC MISSILE

(USSR)

First test-fired in the spring of 1977, the SS-N-18 is now operational aboard most if not all of the Soviet Navy's *Delta-III* class submarines, giving these vessels the ability to strike targets in the continental USA from secure areas in the Barents Sea and Sea of Okhotsk. The US Navy will only be able to match the range of this missile and the similar SS-N-8 when and if the Trident II is deployed in the mid to late 1980s. The Soviet designation for this missile is RSM-50.

Missile Data
Length: 14.1 m
Diameter: 180 cm
Launch weight: unknown
Propulsion: 2-stage liquid propellant
Guidance: unknown
Warhead: Mod 1 3 MIRVs
  Mod 2 nuclear, single
  Mod 3 7 MIRVs
Range: approx 7,500 km (4,050 nm)
Date introduced: Mod 1 1977
  Mod 2 1979
  Mod 3 1979

Status
Operational aboard *Delta-III* class submarines of the Soviet Navy.

SS-NX-20 (NE-04) BALLISTIC MISSILE

(USSR)

A replacement for the SS-N-18 is reported to be already under development, probably to arm the new *Typhoon* class of ballistic-missile submarines. Larger and having a greater throw weight than the SS-N-18, it is reported to be able to carry up to six MIRVs over a range of more than 6,000 km (3,200 nm). Some US reports refer to this missile as the NE-04, which may be its Soviet designation.

ANTI-SHIP MISSILES

CSS-N-1

(CHINA)

China has set up her own production facilities for the Soviet SS-N-2 Styx missile and uses the weapon to arm locally-produced copies of the *Osa* and *Komar* class fast-attack craft, as well as some of the larger Chinese warships. Some sources refer to this missile as the CSS-N-2.

A second pattern of anti-ship missile is also reported to be in production, but this may be an improved Styx rather than an all-new missile.

This is an extended-range surface-to-surface missile system suitable for installation in fast patrol boats or larger vessels. The system comprises a container-launched inertially-guided missile, with automatic altitude control and with an active radar homing system for the terminal phase, backed up by a shipborne target location and fire-control system. The missile has a cylindrical body with a pointed ogival nose and cruciform wings indexed in line with cruciform tail control surfaces. It is powered by a tandem two-stage solid-propellant motor giving it a high subsonic speed.

Computed future target position data are programmed into the missile guidance system before launching and the missile flies on this programmed course to within about 10 km of the target after which the active radar homing system takes control. During flight the missile height is maintained at 2-3 m above the sea surface by a radio altimeter system.

Missile Data
Length: 521 cm
Body diameter: 344 mm
Wing span: 100 cm
Launch weight: 735 kg
Propulsion: solid-propellant rocket
Guidance: inertial plus active radar homing
Warhead: 165 kg HE
Cruising speed: Mach 0.93
Maximum range: 42 km (22.6 nm)

Manufacturer
Aérospatiale (system manufacturer)

Status
In production and in service with, or on order for, a total of at least 20 navies.

Exocet MM38 launch sequence.

EXOCET MM40   (FRANCE)

Aérospatiale is developing this longer-range variant of Exocet as a private venture and is reported to have obtained an export order for the weapon. MM40 uses a longer steel-encased sustainer in place of the shorter light-alloy motor fitted to the MM38 in order to increase the maximum range by a useful 20 per cent or more — some sources credit the new weapon with a range of up to 75 km (40 nm).

This greater range makes greater demands on the seeker head, so Electronique Marcel Dassault (EMD) has given the ADAC X-band device a wider search angle and longer acquisition gate to allow for the greater spread in likely target position which the MM40 would have to cope with at the end of its relatively long flight time.

By using a lightweight glass-fibre launch tube, the company has produced a weapon installation which allows vessels to carry a greater number of rounds than was the case with MM38. The new tube also makes a vehicle-mounted coast-defence variant practical.

Missile Data
Length: 5.8 m
Body diameter: 35 cm
Wing span: 100 cm
Launch weight: 850 kg
Propulsion: solid-propellant rocket
Guidance: inertial plus active radar homing
Warhead: 165 kg HE
Cruising speed: Mach 0.93
Maximum range: 50-75 km (27-40 nm)

Manufacturer
Aérospatiale (system manufacturer)

Status
Under development.

Test firing of Exocet MM40.

SS.11 is a small wire-guided missile developed initially as an anti-tank weapon but suitable as a general-purpose assault weapon and used in some marine installations. Sweden uses the weapon for coastal defence. The current version is the SS.11 B.1.

Missile Data
Length: 120 cm
Body diameter: 16 cm
Wing span: 50 cm
Launch weight: 30 kg
Propulsion: solid-propellant rocket
Guidance: wire guidance command to line-of-sight by joystick controller. Visual tracking
Warhead: HE, armour-piercing or fragmentation
Cruising speed: 580 km/h
Range: 500-3,000 m

Manufacturer
Aérospatiale

Status
In service with nine navies.

Developed by a scaling-up process from the highly-successful SS.11 missile, the SS.12 carries a warhead weighing about four times as much as the earlier missile. The marine version, SS.12 M, was first successfully demonstrated in 1966.

Missile Data
Length: 187 cm
Body diameter: 18 cm (warhead 21 cm)
Wing span: 65 cm
Launch weight: 75 kg
Propulsion: solid-propellant rocket
Guidance: wire-guided command to line-of-sight by joystick controller. Visual tracking
Warhead: 30 kg HE
Range: 6 km (3.2 nm) reached in 32 sec

Manufacturer
Aérospatiale

Status
Operational in several navies.

SS. 12M wire-guided anti-shipping missile.

ANTI-SHIP SUPERSONIC MISSILE (ASSM)

Following preliminary studies carried out since 1974 by Aérospatiale and MBB, later joined by what was then Hawker Siddeley Dynamics, a Memorandum of Understanding covering the development of a next-generation anti-ship missile was signed in April 1977 by the governments of France, Netherlands, Norway, United Kingdom, USA and West Germany. Formal studies were conducted by a new international consortium set up in 1976. Known as ASEM (Anti-Ship Euro-Missile), this was made up of the three companies mentioned earlier. Although initially seen as a weapon for the mid 1980s, the new missile is unlikely to find a significant market until the 1990s in view of the fact that most of the participating nations have invested heavily in existing weapons of the Exocet/Harpoon generation which are unlikely to need replacement until the closing years of the present decade.

Anti-Ship Supersonic Missile (ASSM) is intended to cruise at high supersonic speed, and so will require an air-breathing powerplant. In order to cope with future countermeasures, a dual-mode seeker is thought essential. Television was considered but rejected in favour of passive infra-red homing in order to avoid the need for data links and to produce a fire-and-forget weapon.

Missile Data (provisional)
Launch weight: air launch approx 820 kg
　　　　　　　surface launch approx 970 kg
Propulsion: ramjet or ram-rocket
Guidance: probably strap-down inertial plus active radar and passive infra-red terminal homing
Warhead: 150-200 kg
Cruising speed: approx Mach 2
Maximum range: approx 180 km (97 nm)

Manufacturer
ASEM (Anti-Ship Euro-Missile)

Status
Project-definition phase.

OTOMAT

A long-range surface-to-surface missile system, Otomat is suitable for installation in fast patrol boats or larger vessels. The system comprises a container-launched autopilot-guided missile with automatic altitude control and with an active radar homing system for the terminal phase, backed up by a shipborne target location and fire-control system. The missile has a cylindrical body and pointed nose; its cruciform wings are indexed in line with cruciform tail control surfaces and each carries an air inlet for the turbojet cruise motor at its root. For launching, two lateral jettisonable solid-propellant boosters are mounted in the angles of the wings.

Launched at an angle of 20°, the missile initially climbs to about 150 m then descends, within a distance of about 4 km (2 nm), to its cruising height of 15 m. In this phase it is flying under turbojet power with autopilot navigation and radio altimeter control. When about 12 km (6.5 nm) from the target the active radar homing system takes control and within the last 7 km (3.75 nm) or so the missile executes a programmed climb and steep terminal dive.

The Mk 2 version uses an SMA single-axis radar seeker in place of the two-axis Thomson-CSF device used in the Mk 1 and does not have a terminal climb-and-dive manoeuvre. The Italian Navy version is known as Teseo and incorporates a Marconi Italiana radio command link for over-the-horizon attacks.

Missile Data
Length: 446 cm
Body diameter: 40 cm (forward), 46 cm (over turbojet)
Wing span: 135 cm
Launch weight: 770 kg
Propulsion: solid-propellant rocket boosters plus turbojet
Guidance: autopilot plus active radar seeker
Warhead: 210 kg semi-armour piercing
Maximum range: Mk 1 60-80 km (32-43 nm)
　　　　　　　Mk 2 approx 200 km (approx 108 nm)

Manufacturer
Engins Matra and OTO Melara

Status
Operational. More than 400 rounds ordered by five navies. Egypt has ordered a coastal-defence variant.

One of the few anti-ship missiles to have been tested in combat, Gabriel comes in three different models offering a range of guidance methods. The Israeli Navy prefers semi-active radar since this is less vulnerable to electronic countermeasures than a fire-and-forget active system. As a result, the service probably operates a mixture of Mk 2 and Mk 3 rounds on its vessels. Back-up guidance modes for Gabriel include optical command and home-on-jam.

After launch from its sealed glass-fibre container/launcher, Gabriel climbs to a height of around 100 m under the power of the boost section of its rocket motor. It then descends to around 20 m for the flight to the target under the power of its sustainer, although the final stages of the attack may be flown at an even lower level.

Taiwan has publicly displayed a missile designated Hsiung Feng which was claimed to be of indigenous design, but these appeared to be Gabriel rounds. It is possible that Taiwan builds the weapon under licence, since its navy is a known Gabriel operator.

Missile Data

Length: Mk 1/2 335 cm
Mk 3 approx 350 cm
Body diameter: Mk 1 32.5 cm
Mk 2/3 35 cm
Wing span: 138.5 cm
Launch weight: Mk 1 400 kg
Mk 2 500 kg
Mk 3 over 500 kg
Propulsion: solid-propellant rocket
Guidance: Mk 1/2 inertial plus semi-active radar terminal guidance
Mk 3 inertial plus dual mode (active/semi-active) radar seeker
Warhead: 150-180 kg HE
Cruising speed: Mach 0.7
Maximum range: Mk 1 22 km (14 nm)
Mk 2/3 41 km (26 nm)

Manufacturer
Israel Aircraft Industries

Status
Operational with more than seven navies.

Below: **The turbojet-powered Otomat anti-ship missile.**

Below: **Gabriel Mark 3.**

MARINER

Sistel and SMA are now offering a ship-based version of the Marte anti-ship missile system. By using an SPQ-711 radar — a shipborne version of the APQ-706 radar carried by Marte-armed SH-3D helicopters — the weight of a ship installation complete with two Marte rounds (a slightly modified version of Sea Killer Mk 2), is less than 1,600 kg.

Missile Data
See Sea Killer Mk 2 entry below

SEA KILLER MARK 1

Formerly known as Nettuno, this is a short-range surface-to-surface missile system suitable for installation in fast patrol boats or larger vessels. The system comprises a multiple launcher which can be remotely trained and which carries five missiles pre-packed in launch containers. Missile control is by beam-riding in azimuth and by radio commanded radio altimeter in elevation. If interference precludes beam-riding, optical tracking and radio command can be substituted. The system is designed for use with an X-band gunfire control system modified to provide the radio command and optical (TV) tracking facilities. The missile has a cylindrical light alloy body with an ogival nose section. Control is by movable wings which are indexed in line with the cruciform tail stabilising fins. It is powered by a solid propellant rocket motor which develops 2,000 kg st and burns for 5 secs. After an initial climb the missile descends to within a few metres of the sea surface for the final stages of its flight.

Missile Data
Length: 373 cm
Body diameter: 21 cm
Wing span: 86 cm
Launch weight: 170 kg
Propulsion: solid-propellant rocket
Guidance: beam-riding or radio command
Warhead: 35 kg HE
Cruising speed: subsonic after burn-out
Range: over 10 km (5 nm)
Date introduced: 1969

Manufacturer
Sistel

Status
In service with the Italian Navy on the FPB *Saetta*, otherwise superseded by the Sea Killer Mk 2.

SEA KILLER MARK 2

Formerly known as Vulcano this medium-range surface-to-surface missile system is suitable for installation in fast patrol boats, hydrofoils, gun motor-boats or larger vessels. The system is similar to the earlier Sea Killer Mk 1 but the missile is powered by two solid-propellant motors — a 4,000 kg st booster and a 100 kg st sustainer — and carries a larger warhead. The boost motor is contained in a rear section which is jettisoned after burn-out (about 1.7 secs) and which is fitted with large cruciform wings to stabilise the missile which is unguided during the boost phase. After the boost meter has been jettisoned the sustainer motor is ignited, the missile is gathered to the fire-control radar beam and guided to the target by the same procedures as are used for Sea Killer Mk 1. The missile can be launched from fixed launchers or the quintuple launcher designed for Sea Killer Mk 1.

Missile Data
Length: 470 cm (364 cm without booster)
Body diameter: 21 cm
Wing span: 100 cm
Launch weight: 300 kg
Propulsion: solid-propellant rocket sustainer and booster
Guidance: beam-riding or radio command
Warhead: 70 kg HE
Cruising speed: Mach 0.9
Maximum range: 25 km (13.5 nm)

Manufacturer
Sistel

Status
In service with the Iranian Navy on the *Saam* class frigates. The Mk 2 missile can also be used in the Marte helicopter anti-ship system.

Penguin is a medium-range surface-to-surface missile system intended primarily for installation on fast patrol boats but suitable also for other applications. The system comprises a container-launched, inertially-guided missile, fitted with an infra-red search and homing system for the terminal phase, and requires a back-up data-acquisition and fire-control system. The missile has a cylindrical body with swept cruciform wings which control the flight and which are indexed in line with small swept fins mounted on the tapered nose. It is powered by a two-stage solid-propellant rocket motor. Missiles are supplied pre-packaged in glass-fibre launch containers: these are mounted on fixed launch platforms and connected to the fire-control system by an umbilical connector. After launch the missile follows a predetermined but variable trajectory until within infra-red seeker range of the target; at which point the homing system searches for, locates and locks onto the target, providing terminal guidance for the missile.

The improved and longer-range Mk 2 version is now in production and is being tested by the US Navy as a possible missile armament for light craft. A modified version with smaller wing span is being considered as an air-launch weapon.

Missile Data

Length: 300 cm
Body diameter: 28 cm
Wing span: 140 cm
Launch weight: 340 kg (500 kg including launch container)
Propulsion: solid-propellant rocket
Guidance: inertial plus infra-red homing
Warhead: 120 kg semi-AP, HE. Impact fuze
Cruising speed: Mach 0.8
Maximum range: Mk 1 20 km (10.7 nm)
Mk 2 30 km (16.4 nm)

Manufacturer

A/S Kongsberg Vaapenfabrikk

Status

In service in Royal Norwegian Navy and supplied to Greece and Sweden.

Above left: Sea Killer Mark 2 launched from an Agusta SH-3D helicopter of the Italian Navy.

Left: Launch of Penguin from *Skudd*, a *Storm* class fast missile boat of the Royal Norwegian Navy.

RB 08A

This long-range surface-to-surface cruise missile system is intended for coastal defence or shipborne use on destroyers or larger vessels. The system is based on the French (Aérospatiale, formerly Nord-Aviation) CT20 target drone and comprises a rocket-launched turbojet-powered monoplane with autopilot guidance and (probably) radar homing. The autopilot is programmed with target data up to the moment of launch and maintains course at a constant altitude (after an initial climb) until the homing system takes over for the terminal phase.

Missile Data
Length: 572 m
Body diameter: 66 cm maximum
Wing span: 301 cm
Launch weight: 1,215 kg including 315 kg for rocket booster unit
Propulsion: solid-propellant rocket boosters plus turbojet
Guidance: autopilot plus active radar seeker
Warhead: 250 kg HE
Cruising speed: probably not more than Mach 0.8
Maximum range: 250 km (135 nm)
Date introduced: 1967

Manufacturer
Saab-Scania

Status
Production ceased in 1970. System is now deployed on two *Halland* class destroyers of the Royal Swedish Navy and for coastal defence.

RBS 15

Swedish Navy *Spica* class fast-attack craft are to be armed with this air-breathing subsonic missile, which is scheduled to enter service in 1985. Each vessel will carry eight rounds. Use of an active radar seeker will give the weapon "fire-and-forget" capability, while a radar altimeter will hold the round clear of the water during sea-skimming flight to the target. An air-launched variant will be developed at a later date. Flight trials began early in 1981.

Missile Data
Length: 435 cm
Body diameter: 50 cm
Wing span: 140 cm
Launch weight: 560 kg (excluding boosters)
Propulsion: turbojet plus solid-propellant rocket boosters
Guidance: autopilot plus active radar
Maximum range: ? km

Manufacturer
Saab-Scania

Status
Under development.

Below: RB 08A coast defence cruise missile. **Below right:** RBS 15 air-breathing anti-ship missile.

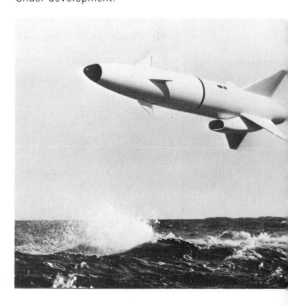

Harpoon is a long-range all-weather, anti-ship cruise missile system. Three systems — air-launched, surface-launched and submarine-launched — all based on the same missile have been developed. The surface-launched version comprises an inertially-guided missile, with an active radar search and homing system for the terminal phase, and a command and launch subsystem which can be used with various launchers backed up by either own ship's or third-party data acquisition devices. This flexibility enables the weapon to be installed on a wide variety of naval vessels ranging upwards in size from patrol hydrofoils. The cylindrical missile has an ogival nose and is fitted with cruciform wings indexed in line with cruciform tail control fins for the main missile and with cruciform fins on the booster assembly which provides initial propulsion: cruise propulsion is by turbojet. During the boost phase the missile executes an unguided climb; after booster separation it is brought on course by the on-board computer and inertial system operating on target data inserted immediately before launch. It then cruises at a low altitude under altimeter control; when it nears the target the active radar homing system is switched on to seek, locate and lock on the target. In the final phase the missile executes a rapid climb-and-dive manoeuvre. The homing radar is frequency agile for ECCM purposes. Suitable missile launchers include those used for ASROC, Tartar and Terrier and a special canister launcher for patrol hydrofoils or other ships not fitted with one of the other launchers.

For underwater launch, the missile is ejected from the submarine's torpedo tube encapsulated in a sealed container. Control fins are deployed from the container to steer it towards the surface at an angle of around 45°. When the container reaches the surface, nose and tail caps are blown off and the round emerges under the power of its solid-propellant booster.

Missile Data
Length: 457 cm (384 cm without booster)
Body diameter: 34 cm
Wing span: 91.4 cm
Launch weight: 667 kg (522 kg without booster)
Propulsion: solid-propellant rocket booster plus turbojet
Guidance: inertial plus active radar seeker
Warhead: 227 kg HE
Cruising speed: Mach 0.85
Maximum range: 110 km (60 nm)

Manufacturer
McDonnell Douglas Astronautics

Status
Operational. More than 1,700 rounds ordered by 13 navies.

Harpoon test fired from US destroyer USS *Knox*.

Standard SSM launch. This missile was developed as an interim weapon pending the introduction of Harpoon.

STANDARD SSM

Formerly known as the Interim Surface-to-Surface Missile (ISSM), the Standard SSM programme was intended to meet an urgent need for an interim weapon capable of being fielded ahead of Harpoon. The immediate objective was met by installing modified versions of Standard aboard vessels already equipped with the surface-to-air variant. These still relied on semi-active radar homing and so were limited to less than horizon range. By adding a passive radar seeker capable of homing on to the radar transmissions of the target vessel, General Dynamics were able to produce the RGM-44D version which still equips vessels of the US and Iranian Navies. However, the servicability of the latter nation's US-supplied weaponry remains doubtful following the withdrawal of US technicians after the Iranian Revolution and the embargo placed by the US Government.

Missile Data
See Standard Missile entry on page 48

Manufacturer
General Dynamics

Status
Operational with the US Navy (six DDGs, six FFGs and four patrol gunboats). Supplied to the Iranian Navy (three destroyers).

Standard missile fired from a US Navy gunboat.

A medium-range surface-to-surface subsonic cruise weapon, also known by the NATO code-name Styx, the SS-N-2 is the most widely-used of the Russian shipborne missiles. It has been operational since 1960, is carried by small fast-attack craft and has been supplied to all the navies of the Warsaw Pact and to those of many other countries. Constructed in the form of a small aircraft, the missile is powered by a solid-propellant jettisonable booster and a sustainer motor which also probably uses a solid propellant. It is launched from an enclosed launcher but differs from some other cell-launched missiles in that the launcher is a re-usable fixture into which the missile is loaded. Several different (but apparently functionally similar) launchers have been observed; and it is believed that two versions of the missile exist. Apart from a suggestion of a slight difference in range performance no differences between these "A" and "B" versions have been reported; but it is thought that the "B" version is the one used (now, at least) by the Warsaw Pact forces. The missile is command-guided and has an active radar homing system.

Missile Data

Length: 650 cm
Body diameter: 75 cm
Wing span: 275 cm
Launch weight: 2,500-3,000 kg
Propulsion: solid-propellant booster plus turbo-jet
Guidance: autopilot or radio command plus infra-red or radar homing
Warhead: approx 400 kg HE
Cruising speed: Mach 0.9
Maximum range: 43 km (23 nm)

Status

Operational on *Komar* (twin-launcher) and *Osa-I* (four-launcher) missile craft with the navies of the Warsaw Pact and many foreign customers. Finland has fitted the weapon to its indigenously-designed missile craft *Isku*; Yugoslavia is fitting it to ten locally-designed Type 211 missile boats; North Korea is fitting it to a new type of missile boat; India has mounted three ex-*Osa* launchers in place of the forward gun turret on the frigates *Trishul* and *Talwar*. A Chinese-built copy equips a wide range of that nation's warships.

SS-N-2 fired from *Osa-I* fast-attack craft of the Russian Navy.

SS-N-3

Since the early 1960s the SS-N-3 (known to NATO as Shaddock) has been one of the most important long-range weapons carried by Soviet warships. Ship designers have shown considerable ingenuity in adapting the weapon to a wide range of surface vessels and submarines. The missile, of which there is probably more than one shipborne version, is extensively deployed in cruisers and submarines of the Soviet Navy. The launcher is a large reloadable cylindrical device which is mounted in single, twin or quadruple installations, fixed or trainable, in the various vessels. On surface ships the twin-antenna Scoop Pair radar is used for initial guidance of Shaddock. The missile appears to have an aeroplane-type configuration and to be propelled by two JATO boosters and a sustainer motor which may be a ramjet or a turbojet. A steep climb after launching appears to be typical of the missile's trajectory and short-range guidance is thought to be pre-programmed with active radar terminal homing. For longer ranges external guidance — for example from aircraft — is assumed to be necessary. The missile has been operational since 1961-2.

Missile Data

Length: approx 1000 cm
Body diameter: approx 100 cm
Wing span: approx 210 cm (wings probably folded within the launch tube)
Launch weight: approx 4,500 kg
Propulsion: solid-propellant rocket booster plus turbojet
Guidance: autopilot with mid-course update plus active radar or infra-red homing
Warhead: nuclear (KT range) or HE
Cruising speed: Mach 1.4
Maximum range: 850 km (460 nm)

Status

Operational only in Soviet Navy. Fitted to *Kynda* cruisers (2 × 4 launchers), *Kresta I* cruisers (2 × 2), E-1 submarines (6 × 1), E-2 (8 × 1), J (2 × 2), W Long Bin (1 × 4) and W Twin Cylinder (2 × 1).

SS-N-3 launchers on *Kynda* class cruiser.

(USSR) SS-N-7

This medium-range sub-surface-to-surface cruise missile is installed on *Charlie* class submarines of the Soviet Navy and capable of being launched below the surface. Few details are available, but the missile and submarine have evidently been the subjects of a comprehensive weapon system design programme. The missile is believed to be supersonic and probably has an active radar homing system: initial guidance is presumably a programmed inertial system linked to the submarine's navigation system. Target detection and identification is reported to be carried out by sonar, identification being achieved by analysis of the acoustic signature. For most of the flight SS-N-7 is believed to operate as a sea-skimmer.

Missile Data
All data approximate.
Length: approx 700 cm
Body diameter: 50-55 cm
Wing span: unknown
Launch weight: approx 3,500 kg
Propulsion: solid-propellant rocket or turbofan
Guidance: autopilot or inertial plus active radar or infra-red homing
Cruising speed: Mach 1.5
Maximum range: 55-60 km (30-32 nm)

Status
Operational since 1969-70 in *Charlie* class nuclear submarines each of which carries eight launching tubes for the missiles in addition to eight 21-inch torpedo tubes.

(USSR) SS-N-9

The only class of Soviet warship known to operate this long-range missile (known to NATO as Siren) is the *Nanuchka* class corvette which carries two triple launchers plus the associated Band Stand radar. Little is known about the weapon, which has never been exported — India's *Nanuchka*s are fitted with two quadruple SS-N-11 launchers in place of the normal armament. The normal combat range of the missile has been estimated as 75-110 km (40-60 nm) but given mid-course updating of the guidance by an aircraft or helicopter, the weapon may remain effective out to 275 km (150 nm).

Missile Data
Length: approx 900 cm
Body diameter: unknown
Wing span: unknown
Launch weight: approx 3,000 kg
Propulsion: not certain; turbojet or turbofan
Guidance: autopilot or inertial with mid-course update plus active radar or infra-red homing
Warhead: nuclear or HE
Cruising speed: probably subsonic
Maximum range: see text

Status
Operational since 1969 aboard *Nanuchka* class corvettes of the Soviet Navy.

Two sets of SS-N-9 triple launch tubes are visible on either side of this Soviet Navy Nanuchka-class patrol craft.

SS-N-11 (USSR)

Believed to be an improved version of the earlier SS-N-2 Styx missile, this weapon is now often referred to as the SS-N-2 (Mod). No photographs of the missile have been published so far and the data given here must be regarded as provisional.

Missile Data

Length: approx 650 cm
Body diameter: unknown
Wing span: unknown
Launch weight: approx 3,000 kg
Propulsion: probably solid-propellant rocket boosters plus turbofan
Guidance: inertial plus active radar and/or infra-red homing
Warhead: approx 500 kg HE
Cruising speed: Mach 0.9
Maximum range: 50 km (27 nm)

Status

In service with the Soviet Navy aboard *Osa-II* class FPBs (4 × 1), Modified *Kashin* class destroyers (4 × 1), *Kildin* class destroyers (4 × 1) and *Matka* class FPBs (2 × 1); Iraqi Navy (*Osa-II*); Indian Navy aboard *Nanuchka* class corvettes (2 × 4); ordered by Finnish Navy (*Osa-II*).

SS-NX-19 (USSR)

These silo-launched anti-ship missiles are carried by *Kirov* class battlecruisers and are understood to have a range of around 300 or 400 km.

SS-N-12 (USSR)

First deployed aboard *Kiev* class carriers but due to enter service on a new class of guided missile cruiser under construction as this book was in preparation, the SS-N-12 may be based on the SS-N-3 Shaddock. The system operates in conjunction with a retractable bow-mounted radar known to NATO as Trap Door.

Missile Data

Length: approx 1,000 cm
Wing span: approx 250 cm
Launch weight: approx 5,000 kg
Propulsion: turbojet plus solid-propellant rocket boosters
Guidance: cruise: probably autopilot with mid-course update
attack: probably active radar seeker
Warhead: nuclear or HE, approx 1,000 kg
Cruising speed: Mach 2.5
Maximum range: 500 km (270 nm)

Foredeck of *Kiev* showing containers housing SS-N-12 missiles.

SURFACE-TO-AIR MISSILES

CSA-? (CHINA)

The frigates of the *Kiangtung* class are reported to carry a new pattern of surface-to-air missile, but some sources believe that this has not proved particularly successful and may not be installed in future vessels. The system may be derived from the Soviet SA-3 GOA which has been supplied to several nations known to have good relations with Peking.

SEA SPARROW (CANADA)

This system is intended for use in both surface-to-surface and surface-to-air engagements. It uses the AIM-7E2 version of the Sparrow III missile (Raytheon) which is operational in other systems in various countries. In the Canadian system the missile is launched from a four-missile support pylon on an extendable cantilever beam.

Missiles can be fired singly or in rapid succession, automatic pre-launch commands being supplied electrically. Semi-automatic power loading provides rapid recycling and launching.

A Signaal radar and M22 fire-control system capable of handling surface and airborne targets simultaneously is an integral part of the missile system.

Missile Data
See NATO Sea Sparrow entry on page 47

Manufacturer
System contractor: Raytheon Canada

Status
Operational as a dual installation in *Iroquois* class destroyers and as a single installation in the replenishment ships *Preserver* and *Protector* of the Canadian Armed Forces.

Canadian *Iroquois* class destroyer armed with Sea Sparrow missiles.

CATULLE

(FRANCE)

Catulle is the naval equivalent of a land-mobile surface-to-air weapon system called Javelot which has been in development for some years. The system comprises a multi-tube, gun-effect rocket launcher capable of firing salvoes of rockets with a predetermined dispersion, an acquisition radar, a fire-control radar and a digital computer.

Detailed information is in short supply, but the launcher is believed to consist of a roughly rectangular array of 96 launch tubes from which numerous salvoes of rockets can be fired, before reloading is necessary, with a gap of 2-4 secs between salvoes. Effective range is believed to be about 1,500 m and calibre is 40 mm.

Manufacturer
System: Thomson-CSF

Status
Under development.

(FRANCE)

MASURCA

Masurca is a long-range tandem two-stage anti-aircraft weapon deployed on some French naval vessels. The missile has a cylindrical body with a pointed nose and pivoted cruciform tail control surfaces indexed in line with long-chord narrow wings. Powered by solid-propellant booster and sustainer motors, it is launched from a twin launcher and carries a proximity-fused high-explosive warhead. It can intercept supersonic targets at ranges of 40 km (21.5 nm) or more.

Two types of guidance are employed: the Mk 2 Mod 2 missile is guided by radio command and the Mk 2 Mod 3 uses semi-active radar homing. Externally the two versions are virtually identical and the complete shipboard installation — which includes an independent fire-control system for each twin launcher and a three-dimensional radar system — is designed to handle the two types simultaneously: it can also track and control two radio command missiles simultaneously, long-range tracking being aided by a missile-borne transponder.

Missile Data
Length: 8.6 m
Body diameter: 40 cm
Wing span: 77 cm
Launch weight: Mod 2 1,850 kg
Mod 3 2,080 kg
Propulsion: solid-propellant booster and sustainer motors
Guidance: Mod 2 radio command
Mod 3 semi-active radar homing
Warhead: 48 kg HE
Maximum range: Mod 2 40 km (21.5 nm)
Mod 3 45 km (24 nm)

Manufacturer
DTCN/ECAN Ruelle

Status
Both types are operational in the cruiser *Colbert* and the *Suffren* class destroyers of the French Navy.

Masurca missile on launcher.

By opting to use a variant of the widely-deployed Crotale surface-to-air missile, the French Navy has been able to develop a naval point-defence missile system with a minimum of trouble and cost compared with that likely to be faced in tackling an all-new system.

Like the land-based weapon, Naval Crotale uses semi-automatic command to line-of-sight (SACLOS) guidance commands from a radar tracker to steer an 85 kg missile at ranges of up to 8.5 km (4.6 nm). Target designation data can be accepted from the ship's Central Operations Room or Fire Control Room. The ship's search radars, optical or infra-red trackers or other systems can be used to lay the Naval Crotale fire unit onto the target. Only one operator is required at the Crotale console and the launcher turret carries eight ready-for-use rounds as well as the tracking and command link antennae and other sensors.

A two-round salvo can be fired within 2.5 secs, improving the 0.75 kill probability which the manufacturer claims for a single shot. After launch the missile is automatically gathered onto the line-of-sight by an infra-red system, and from then on is guided by commands from the ship-based radar tracker although television tracking can be used if necessary at low angles of fire.

Naval Crotale is scheduled to be fitted to a range of French Navy warships including *Georges Leygues* class corvettes and *Tourville* class frigates.

Missile Data
Length: 293 cm
Body diameter: 15.6 cm
Wing span: 54 cm
Launch weight: 85.1 kg
Propulsion: solid-propellant rocket
Guidance: SACLOS with radar or TV tracking
Warhead: 15 kg HE
Maximum range: 8.5 km (4.6 nm)
Altitude limit: maximum 3,600 m
minimum 500 m

Manufacturer
System: Thomson-CSF
Missile: Engins Matra

Status
Operational aboard vessels of the French Navy. Ordered by several overseas customers including Saudi Arabia.

Naval Crotale fired from a ship of the French Navy.

NATO 65

NATO is considering the development of a vertically launched anti-aircraft missile with an active radar seeker for service in the early 1990s. Project-definition and development contracts were expected to be awarded during 1981 to an industrial team led by British Aerospace, Thomson-CSF and AEG-Telefunken. The weapon may have a range of 10-15 km and use semi-active radar mid-course guidance plus active radar terminal homing in the final stages of flight, but this has not been confirmed. Target acquisition and tracking will probably be by means of a 3-D pulse-Doppler radar plus an infra-red surveillance sensor and electro-optical tracker.

ALBATROS

This weapon system combines the medium-range performance of surface-to-air missiles with the high firepower of conventional naval armament. Following trials of the Mk 1 configuration aboard the Italian Navy vessel *Aviere* in the early 1970s, the definitive Mk 2 version has now entered service on the *Lupo* class frigates. The system has sold well on the export market and is available in a range of variants to suit the customer's needs, since each is likely to request a different gun fire-control system. Variants announced to date are:

Designation	Gun fire-control system
Mk 2 Mod 3	Elsag NA10
Mk 2 Mod 5	Elsag NA22
Mk 2 Mod 7	Elsag NA30
Mk 2 Mod 8	Ferranti WSA-4
Mk 2 Mod 9	Hollandse Signaalapparaten WM 25

Each is obtainable in single or double-ended configurations.

Albatros was originally designed to use the Sea Sparrow missile but can also use the Italian-developed Aspide missile. Performance details of both may be obtained under the relevant entries in this volume.

Manufacturer
Selenia — Industrie Elettroniche Associate

Status
Operational aboard Italian and foreign warships. Seven navies have ordered the system.

ASPIDE

Aspide is a high-performance multi-purpose missile developed for use both in an air-to-air role and in such shipborne weapon systems as Albatros — there being slight differences in dimensions between the two versions. The following data apply to the surface-launched version.

Missile Data
Length: 370 cm
Body diameter: 203 mm
Wing span: 80 cm
Fin span: 64 cm
Launch weight: 220 kg
Propulsion: single-stage solid-propellant rocket motor
Guidance: semi-active radar homing
Warhead: 35 kg HE

Manufacturer
Selenia — Industrie Elettroniche Associate

Status
Operational. First batch of production missiles ordered in 1977.

Albatros fired from 8-cell fibreglass launcher.

VANESSA   (ITALY)

An industrial team headed by OTO Melara is currently working on a new point-defence missile system for deployment in the late 1980s. This is expected to be a relatively large subsonic weapon using command to line-of-sight guidance and a large warhead fitted with an advanced type of proximity fuse. The system will be fitted to *Maestrale* class frigates and *Garibaldi* class carriers.

SEACAT   (UK)

This widely-exported point-defence weapon is now in service with 16 navies and is still in production. The basic GWS20 adopted by the Royal Navy used a "dustbin" housing for the operator who tracked the round after launch through binoculars, sending steering commands by means of a thumb-operated joystick control to keep the round on the line-of-sight to the target. The more recent GWS22 links a tracking radar to the aimer's sight, and the weapon has also been linked in various installations to foreign radars such as the Contraves Sea Hunter and the Hollandse Signaalapparaten M 40 series. A lightweight three-round launcher has also been developed for light craft such as minesweepers and fast-attack craft and this has been purchased by Brazil and Iran.

Latest modification to the system has been the development of a height-control system to allow the weapon to be used against low-level targets including light craft and sea-skimming missiles. A new wing containing the height sensor replaces one of the normal wings. By sending commands to the autopilot, it prevents the round from ditching while in low-level flight. A two-round installation with fixed launcher has also been devised to allow these modified missiles to be used as surface-to-surface weapons on small patrol craft.

Missile Data
Length: 147 cm
Body diameter: 19 cm
Wing span: 65 cm
Launch weight: 63 kg
Propulsion: solid-propellant rocket
Guidance: command to line-of-sight
Warhead: HE
Maximum range: approx 5 km (2.7 nm)

Manufacturer
Shorts

Status
Operational aboard warships of the Royal Navy and the navies of Argentina, Australia, Bangladesh, Brazil, Chile, India, Iran, Libya, Malaysia, Netherlands, New Zealand, Sweden, Thailand and Venezuela.

Test firing of Seacat during trials of new wing containing height sensor.

After a protracted development programme, the Sea Dart area-defence missile is now fully operational. Powered by a solid-propellant booster and Rolls-Royce Odin ramjet sustainer, it uses semi-active radar homing in conjunction with a proportional navigation system whose law can be changed in flight. Target tracking and illumination are handled by a Marconi Radar systems Type 909 radar, and the missile is fired from a twin-rail launcher. Handling and loading of rounds is fully automatic.

The standard Royal Navy version described above is the GWS30 but development work on the Sea Dart Mk 2 GWS31 has already begun. The new missile will have miniaturised guidance and control electronics, leaving more internal volume for fuel. Other suggested improvements include larger wings and control surfaces to improve manoeuvrability and a new solid-propellant booster with thrust-vector control.

British Aerospace is also developing Lightweight Sea Dart, which will be suitable for installation in vessels as small as 300 tons. This version would substitute the Marconi ST804 tracker/illuminator for the existing Type 909 radar, or would rely on the fitting of a continuous-wave target-illuminator slaved to or fitted to the mounting of an existing radar tracker. Standard Sea Dart Mk 1 rounds would be carried in fixed container/launchers mounted on the ship's deck. Performance of such a system would be dependant on the performance of the radar tracker used, Sea Dart having sufficient range to intercept any target which a lightweight tracker can engage. In addition to its regular surface-to-air role, Lightweight Sea Dart may also be used as an anti-ship weapon.

Missile Data
Length: 440 cm
Body diameter: 42 cm
Wing span: 91 cm
Launch weight: 550 kg
Propulsion: solid-propellant rocket booster plus ramjet
Guidance: semi-active radar homing
Warhead: HE (fragmentation)
Maximum range: over 80 km (43 nm)
Altitude limit: maximum 25,000 m
minimum 30 m

Manufacturer
British Aerospace Dynamics

Status
Operational with the Royal Navy on *Invincible* class V/STOL carriers, *Sheffield* class (Type 42) destroyers and a single Type 82 destroyer. To be deployed on *Manchester* class improved Type 42 destroyers. Also used by the Argentinian Navy (two Type 42 destroyers).

Sea Dart surface-to-air missiles.

SEAFOX

The Hunting Engineering solution to defending warships from attacks by sea-skimming missiles is Seafox, a system which will engage the incoming round at very close range using a salvo of unguided missiles.

Marconi Radar is developing an advanced surveillance/tracking radar which will detect the target, then track its flight path. The radar will pass information to a Ferranti computer which will in turn aim the Vickers launchers.

Use of a large warhead and advanced proximity fuse should give Seafox the lethality required to stop anti-ship missiles, either by detonating the warhead or by causing massive structural damage. The system is a private venture and is intended to be about half the cost of an equivalent guided-missile system.

Manufacturer
Hunting Engineering (lead contractor, rocket)
Ferranti (computers)
Marconi Space and Defence Systems (radar, proximity fuse)
Vickers Shipbuilding (launch complexes)

Status
Private venture.

SEASLUG

This long-range beam-riding surface-to-air missile system has been in service with the Royal Navy since 1961. It is fitted in the *County* class destroyers, and is launched from a twin-ramp launcher which is commanded by the fire-control system and reloaded from a between-decks magazine.

There are two versions of the missile, the Mk 2 having a longer range and better low-altitude performance. Both missiles can be used against surface targets; but again the performance of the Mk 2 is superior to that of the Mk 1.

The unconventional appearance of this missile results from the forward mounting of four wrap-around solid-propellant boosters. The missile proper is cylindrical with a pointed ogival nose-cone and cruciform fixed mid-body wings indexed in line with cruciform pivoted tail control surfaces.

Missile Data
Length: 610 cm
Body diameter: 41 cm
Wing span: 144 cm
Launch weight: approx 1,000 kg
Propulsion: four wrap-around solid-propellant booster rockets plus solid-propellant rocket sustainer
Guidance: radar beam-riding using Type 901 target-tracking radar
Warhead: 35 kg HE
Maximum range: minimum 45 km
Altitude limit: maximum 15,000 m minimum unknown

Manufacturer
British Aerospace Dynamics

Status
Being phased out of Royal Navy service. Only three of the Mk 2-equipped vessels were operational in April 1981.

SEAWOLF

Designed for rapid-reaction defence against aircraft and missile attack, Seawolf is suitable in its current GWS25 form for use in vessels of down to 3,000 tons displacement. The missile is guided in flight by signals from the Marconi Radar Type 910 tracker, a differential tracking system which tracks both missile and target, measuring the displacement between the missile and the tracker-to-target sightline. Tracking is normally by radar, with television back-up for use at the lowest angles of elevation.

Targets are initially detected by the Type 967 and 968 radars, an air-surveillance and surface-surveillance radars with antennae mounted back-to-back in a single rotating assembly. Six rounds are carried ready for use in a steerable launcher, which is manually loaded. In order to achieve the required reaction time, all phases of the engagement are automatic once the target has been identified as hostile.

The system, though successful, is both expensive and bulky, so BAe has developed and test-fired a lightweight version. This uses an Anglo-Dutch VM.40 tracker based on the Hollandse Signaalapparaten STIR tracker and a twin-rail launcher capable of being reloaded from below deck.

Missile Data
Length: 190 cm
Body diameter: 18 cm
Wing span: 56 cm
Launch weight: 82 kg
Propulsion: solid-propellant rocket
Guidance: semi-automatic command to line-of-sight
Warhead: 13.4 kg HE
Maximum range: 5 km (2.7 nm)

Manufacturer
British Aerospace Dynamics

Status
Operational on Type 22 frigates of the Royal Navy. Being retrofitted onto ten *Leander* class frigates.

Seaslug launcher on HMS *Kent*.

Seawolf close-range anti-missile/aircraft missile.

SLAM

SLAM denotes Submarine-Launched Air Missile System. It has been developed by Vickers to provide submarines or light craft with an effective short-range defence against other surface craft and helicopters.

The missile chosen as the basis of the system is Blowpipe, which was originally developed as a man-portable AA missile. Vickers have developed a special launcher for SLAM comprising six missiles grouped round a central electronics and TV unit which is used as the "eye" of the system for missile guidance. For submarine installation this unit is raised into action from a pressure vessel in which it is housed when submerged. Target acquisition is by means of the submarine's attack periscope with the azimuth of which the launcher unit is automatically aligned when its mast is raised. This brings the target into the view of a remote operator by means of the TV system; whereafter the operator tracks the target and fires and guides the missile (which is automatically gathered to the line-of-sight) by remote control.

Missile Data

Length: 140 cm
Body diameter: 7.6 cm
Wing span: 27.5 cm
Launch weight: 11 kg
Propulsion: solid-propellant rocket
Guidance: infra-red autogathering, then command to line-of-sight
Warhead: 2.2 kg HE
Maximum range: minimum 3 km (1.6 nm)
Altitude limit: maximum 2,000 m
minimum unknown

Manufacturer
System: Vickers
Missile: Shorts

Status
Operational on submarines of at least two navies.

SLAM trials installations on a Royal Navy submarine's fin.

44

Aegis is a shipborne area-defence system primarily concerned with ship defence against anti-ship cruise missiles and high-performance aircraft. Its special feature is its elaborate multi-function multiple phased-array radar (AN/SPY-1) and associated computer-controlled data handling and fire-control system.

The detailed operation of this system is outside the scope of this book, however, and it is sufficient to note the capability of the system to launch and control the SM-2 surface-to-air missile from the fully-automatic Mk 26 dual-purpose launcher which can also be used to launch ASROC.

SM-2 is a special Aegis version of the Standard missile and is a semi-active radar homing device with provision for mid-course command guidance. Available details of this missile will be found under the Standard heading. A more advanced missile is expected to be added to Aegis in due course. When this happens the Talos system, in particular, will be retired from service.

Trials of Aegis began in 1974 aboard the trials ship *Norton Sound*, and by mid-1977 had been successfully completed. Both the AN/SPY-1 radar and SM-2 missile had then completed development, so the US Navy placed a $ 224 million contract with RCA covering the construction and integration of the first operational Aegis system, due to go to sea in 1983 aboard the lead ship of the DDG-47 class. Although originally rated as destroyers, these vessels are now to be designated CG-47 class cruisers.

Manufacturer
System contractor: RCA Government and Commercial Systems

Status
Under development for the US Navy. The system is due to be fitted to CG-47 class cruisers.

Aegis will arm the new CG-47 class cruisers.

BASIC POINT-DEFENCE MISSILE SYSTEM

(USA)

One of several shipborne anti-aircraft systems based on versions of the Sparrow air-to-air missile, the BPDMS was assembled as a working system from existing hardware with a minimum of new development. The AIM-7E Sparrow III missile is launched from a modified eight-cell ASROC launcher mounted on a 3-inch gun mounting. Missile guidance is by CW semi-active radar homing; target data from the ship's combat information centre are supplied to a manually-operated fire-control system; and the target is acquired and illuminated for homing guidance by a director/illuminator radar controlled manually by handlebar controls. Low-angle engagements are possible and the weapon can be used against surface targets.

Manufacturer
System Contractor: Raytheon

Status
In service in the USN since 1972.

BPDMS launch.

The NATO version of Sea Sparrow uses a new pattern of eight-cell launcher, a fire-control system using digital computers and a powered director-illuminator. This fires the RIM-7H, a Sparrow variant fitted with folding fins, although the improved RIM-7M with a monopulse seeker head is currently under development.

The programme was set up in 1968 with the signing of a Memorandum of Understanding between Belgium, Denmark and Italy, but the Netherlands and West Germany subsequently joined the project. First test-firing took place in 1972, and the system entered production in the latter half of 1973.

Installations of the weapon aboard some high-value USN vessels are to be improved by the addition of the Hughes Mk 23 Target Acquisition System — a pulse-Doppler system which automatically detects and tracks targets as they come over the horizon.

Missile Data
Length: 65 cm
Body diameter: 20 cm
Wing span: 102 cm
Launch weight: 205 kg
Propulsion: solid-propellant rocket
Guidance: continuous-wave semi-active radar homing
Warhead: 30 kg HE
Maximum range: 18 km (9.7 nm)
Altitude limit: maximum 5,000 m
minimum 5 m

Manufacturer
Raytheon. To be licence-built in Japan by Mitsubishi

Status
Operational aboard vessels of the US Navy and those of Norway, Belgium and the Netherlands. Also ordered by the Danish, German and Japanese navies.

Nato Sea Sparrow launched from an amphibious assault ship.

ROLLING AIRFRAME MISSILE

Denmark, West Germany and the United States are sponsoring the development of a lightweight missile capable of protecting warships from missile attack. Rolling Airframe Missile (RAM) uses the Sidewinder rocket motor coupled to a seeker derived from that fitted to the Stinger man-portable surface-to-air missile. Guidance in the early stages of flight will be by passive radar homing, switching to infra-red homing as the range closes. Production is due to begin in 1983 and the round can be fired either from the custom-designed EX-31 launcher or from the cells of a standard Sea Sparrow launcher.

Missile Data
Length: 280 cm
Body diameter: 12.7 cm
Launch weight: 70 kg
Propulsion: solid-propellant rocket
Guidance: passive radar and infra-red homing
Warhead: HE
Maximum range: 6 km (3.2 nm)

Manufacturer
General Dynamics

Status
Under development.

SEA CHAPARRAL

This naval version of the Chaparral point-defence missile uses a slightly modified launcher capable of being directed either by a gunner or by remote control by the parent vessel's fire-control system. In all other respects, it is similar to the standard land-based weapon. Sea Chaparral was offered to Taiwan in 1980 but no deployments have been reported.

Missile Data
Length: 291 cm
Body diameter: 12.7 cm
Wing span: 64 cm
Launch weight: 84 kg
Propulsion: solid-propellant rocket
Guidance: infra-red homing
Warhead: 5 kg continuous-rod
Maximum range: over 3 km (1.6 nm)

Manufacturer
Ford Aerospace

STANDARD (SM-1) MISSILE

First conceived as a two-model range of replacements for the Terrier and Tartar, the Standard missiles have now evolved into a wide range of weapons, the main naval variants of which are listed below. Most are available in Medium Range (missile only) and Extended Range (missile plus booster) versions.

RIM-66A STANDARD (MR) original replacement for Improved Tartar.

RIM-66B STANDARD (MR) similar to the above but with improved rocket motor.

RGM-66E STANDARD SSM (ARM) passive-radar homing missile for surface-to-surface use.

RIM-67A STANDARD (ER) replacement for Terrier.

Subsequent development work has resulted in the much-improved Standard SM-2 (see separate entry).

Missile Data
Length: MR 447 cm
ER 798 cm
Body diameter: 35 cm
Wing span: 91 cm
Launch weight: MR 581 kg
ER 1,066 kg
Propulsion: solid-propellant rocket (with booster in ER version)
Guidance: semi-active radar homing
Warhead: HE
Maximum range: MR 30 km (16 nm)
ER 56 km (30 nm)
Altitude limit: maximum greater than 20,000 m for both versions
minimum unknown

Manufacturer
General Dynamics

Status
In service with the US Navy, Spanish Navy and other former Tartar/Terrier operators.

Sea Chaparral surface-to-air missile system.

RIM/67A Standard.

STANDARD (SM-2) MISSILE (USA)

Developed for use with the Aegis system (see page 45), this improved Standard variant is available in Medium Range (missile only) and Extended Range (missile plus booster) versions. The use of a command mid-course guidance system which operates in conjunction with a built-in inertial reference unit, plus the use of a new monopulse seeker in place of the conically-scanned unit carried by SM-1 rounds allows the weapon to fly a much-refined tragectory. This extends the range of the medium-range version by 60 per cent and more than doubles the range of the extended-range missile. Under the Block 2 programme, the SM-2 is to be fitted with an improved rocket motor to give greater speed and altitude performance, and a modified autopilot to cope with this performance boost and to give greater stability under mid-course guidance and to increase manoeuvrability during the terminal homing stage of flight. G-47 cruisers and other vessels will fire SM-2s from the Martin Marietta EX-41 vertical launching system, but vessels retrofitted with the weapon will retain conventional launchers.

Missile Data
Length: MR 447 cm
ER 798 cm
Body diameter: 35 cm
Wing span: 91 cm
Launch weight: MR 581 kg
ER 1,066 kg
Propulsion: solid-propellant rocket (with booster in ER version)
Guidance: semi-active radar homing
Warhead: HE
Maximum range: MR 48 km (26 nm)
ER 121 km (65 nm)
Altitude limit: maximum over 20,000 m for both versions
minimum unknown

Manufacturer
General Dynamics

Status
Entering service with the US Navy.

Standard SM-2.

One of the few NATO shipborne surface-to-air missiles to have been used in action, successfully intercepting targets at a range of some 110 km (59.5 nm), Talos is a large long-range missile installed on some cruisers of the USN. The basic missile employs beam-riding guidance with semi-active terminal homing: in recent versions the semi-active CW guidance uses an interferometer technique and in another version an anti-radiation homing head is fitted — possibly for surface-to-surface applications.

The missile comprises a solid-propellant jettisonable booster and a ramjet sustainer, the whole being contained in a cylindrical body tapered slightly towards the ramjet air intake in the nose in which is mounted a conical centre body. Control is by pivoted cruciform wings indexed in line with cruciform tail fins, which in turn are in line with the fins of the booster. The missile is launched from a twin launcher which is electrically operated and commanded by the fire-control system.

Missile Data
Length: 640 cm (plus 313 cm for the booster)
Body diameter: 76 cm
Wing span: 290 cm
Launch weight: 3,175 kg
Warhead: HE or nuclear
Speed: Mach 2.5
Range: over 120 km (65 nm)
Altitude limit: over 26,500 m
Date introduced: 1959

Manufacturer
System contractor: Bendix

Status
In service in the USN and expected to remain in service until replaced by Aegis when the latter has a longer-range missile than the SM-2.

Talos missile on twin launchers.

TARTAR

(USA)

This medium-range missile is still in widespread service in NATO navies and elsewhere providing primary air defence for ships of destroyer size and secondary defence for some larger vessels. A fully-automatic magazine handling and loading system is employed and missiles are fired from an electrically-driven remotely-commanded twin launcher. Guidance is by semi-automatic radar homing.

The Tartar missile has a cylindrical body with an ogival nose and long narrow cruciform fixed wings almost touching the wider tail control surfaces.

Missile Data
Length: 460 cm
Body diameter: 35 cm
Wing span: 107 cm
Launch weight: 680 kg
Propulsion: solid-propellant rocket
Guidance: semi-active radar
Warhead: HE
Maximum range: minimum 16 km (8.6 nm)
Altitude limit: maximum 12,000 m
minimum 300 m

Manufacturer
Raytheon

Status
No longer in production and being replaced by Standard-1 (MR), Tartar is still in service with the USN and with the Australian, French, Iranian, Italian, Japanese, Netherlands, Spanish and West German navies.

Tartar launched from guided-missile destroyer USS *Sampson*.

Operational since 1956, Terrier has been the subject of almost continuous development and improvement and is still in service. It is gradually being replaced by the Standard missile. Current systems are generally those known as Advanced Terrier which is visually distinguishable from the early versions by the change of wing planform from the original cropped-delta shape to the current strake-like outline.

Structurally the missile is of tandem two-stage design with a cylindrical body and ogival nose. The booster stage is of larger diameter than the main missile and has cruciform fins indexed in line with the missile tail control surfaces which in turn lie immediately to the rear of the missile wings.

Guidance is by a beam-riding system with semi-active radar terminal homing and the missile is launched from an electrically-operated remotely-controlled twin launcher which in some installations is shared with ASROC.

Missile Data
Length: 823 cm (missile 460 cm, booster 363 cm)
Body diameter: 30.5 cm
Wing span: 157 cm
Launch weight: 1,360 kg
Propulsion: solid-propellant rocket booster and sustainer
Guidance: cruise, radar beam-riding; attack, semi-active radar homing
Warhead: HE (nuclear in RIM-2D)
Maximum range: 35 km (19 nm)
Altitude limit: maximum 20,000 m
minimum unknown

Manufacturer
General Dynamics

Status
In service with the USN and in the navies of Italy and the Netherlands.

The long-serving Terrier missile on board USS *Canberra*.

SA-N-1 GOA

This missile is known by the NATO code-name Goa and is well-known as the SA-3 land-mobile missile which has figured largely in the Arab-Israeli wars. The missile is installed in many of the larger warships of the Soviet Navy on roll stabilised twin launchers mounted on top of magazines from which they are reloaded vertically.

Powered by a booster and sustainer, the missile proper is cylindrical and slim with relatively large cruciform fixed wings at the rear and small cropped-delta control surfaces on the tapered nose. The booster is short, larger in diameter and furnished with rectangular fins indexed in line with the other control surfaces. Some missiles have an additional set of small tail fins between the booster and the second-stage wings which appear to be furnished with trailing-edge control surfaces: it is thought that this is the more modern version of the missile.

Associated with all installations is the radar complex known as Peel Group.

Missile Data

Length: 590 cm
Body diameter: 45 cm (body), 70 cm (booster)
Wing span: 122 cm
Launch weight: 600 kg
Propulsion: booster, solid-propellant;
sustainer, probably solid-propellant
Guidance: radio command
Warhead: 60 kg HE
Maximum range: 30-35 km (16-19 nm)
Altitude limit: maximum 10,000-15,000 m
minimum approx 100 m
Date introduced: 1961-62

Status

Widely deployed aboard Soviet Navy vessels incluing the *Kanin*, *Kashin*, *Kotlin*, *Kresta* and *Knynda* classes. Also in service aboard Soviet-supplied warships of the Polish and Indian navies.

SA-N-1 missiles aboard *Kashin* class destroyer of the Russian Navy.

SA-N-1 missiles on launcher.

(USSR)

SA-N-2 is the US alphanumeric code for the shipborne version of the missile known by the NATO code-name Guideline.

This long-range anti-aircraft missile, which has for many years been the principal field AA weapon of the Soviet forces and has been used in action extensively in Vietnam and the Middle East, has been installed in only one Russian ship, the cruiser *Dzerzhinski*, on a twin mounting.

Since in order to make this installation a triple 6-inch gun turret (X position) was removed, it is scarcely surprising that the SA-N-3 installation has been left in position: the absence of other installations of what is clearly otherwise a well-regarded missile, however, makes it fairly clear that the experiment was a failure. The most probable reason for this is that, even when fired from a stable structure on land, the Guideline missile is difficult to gather to the desired flight path: it is said, indeed, that if it is not brought into the radar beam in the first 6 secs it will not be acquired at all. Clearly, the motion of a ship in a heavy sea would make this process even more difficult. The associated Fan Song E radar must also present installation difficulties — especially on smaller ships.

Missile Data
Length: 10.7 m
Body diameter: 50 cm (missile), 70 cm (booster)
Wing span: 170 cm (missile), 220 cm (booster)
Launch weight: 2,300 kg
Propulsion: booster, solid-propellant rocket; sustainer, liquid-propellant rocket
Guidance: radio command
Warhead: 130 kg HE fragmentation
Maximum range: 40-50 km (21.6-27 nm)
Altitude limit: maximum 18,000 m
minimum approx 300 m

Status
Installed on one vessel but probably no longer operational.

(USSR)

First vessels to be deployed with this second-generation surface-to-air missile were the helicopter carrier *Moskva* and the *Kresta II* class cruisers. The system uses the Head Light radar and a multi-purpose twin-rail launcher. When a Seawolf-configuration missile was sighted on the rails of this launcher, the weapon was at first assumed to be Goblet, but it now seems that it was an SA-N-14 anti-submarine missile, the other system fired from this pattern of launcher. In the same way that the land-based SA-3 was navalised to create the SA-N-1, the SA-6 Gainful was probably developed to produce the SA-N-3 Goblet, but this has yet to be positively confirmed.

Status
Operational on *Kiev* class aircraft carriers, *Moskva* class helicopter carriers, plus the *Kara* and *Kresta II* class cruisers. All carry two launchers.

SA-N-3 Goblet launchers visible front centre of Kresta II guided missile cruiser, *Vassili Chapaev*.

For point-defence of its warships, the Soviet Navy depends on the SA-N-4, a navalised version of the vehicle-mounted SA-8 Gecko. Virtually a Soviet-bloc equivalent to the French Naval Crotale, this weapon is thought to use command guidance.

The launcher is a twin-rail retractable unit installed in a silo. When within range of prying eyes, the Soviet Navy is careful to keep the launcher retracted — although the installation has been photographed on at least one occasion. In the early days of operational deployment, the associated Pop Group radar was kept covered by canvas screens, but has since been seen often enough to reveal its close relationship with the radars on the SA-8 vehicle. Unlike the latter, it has only a single secondary antenna flanking the main unit.

Missile Data

Length: 320 cm
Body diameter: 21 cm
Wing span: 64 cm
Launch weight: 180-200 kg
Propulsion: solid-propellant rocket
Guidance: radio command
Warhead: 40-50 kg HE
Maximum range: 12 km (6.5 nm)
Altitude limit: maximum 6,000 m
　　　　　　　　minimum 50 m

Status

Operational with the Soviet Navy aboard *Kiev* class aircraft carriers, *Kirov* class battlecruisers, *Kara* class cruisers, modified *Sverdlov* class command ships, *Krivak* class destroyers, *Nanuchka, Grisha I* and *Koni* class corvettes, *Ropucha* class assault craft, *Ivan Rogov* class amphibious-warfare ships and *Berezina* class replenishment ships. Operational with the Indian Navy aboard *Nanuchka* class corvettes.

'Dustbin lid' cover of the SA-N-4 weapon system is immediately forward of the guns on this *Krivak* class destroyer.

(USSR)

SA-N-5

This designation has been reported for naval installations of the SA-7 Grail man-portable anti-aircraft missile. The weapon has been deployed on a simple pivoted mount aboard *Osa-I* and *II* missile boats and on *Shershen* class Torpedo-boats. It is not known whether the naval version uses the Mk 2 version of the missile or the earlier Mk 1. Both are manually directed by the gunner and fired once the infra-red seeker has locked on to the target.

Missile Data
Length: 135 cm
Body diameter: 7 cm
Launch weight: 9.2 kg
Propulsion: solid-propellant rocket
Guidance: infra-red passive homing
Warhead: 2.5 kg HE fragmentation
Maximum range: 3.6 km
Altitude limit: maximum 1,500 m
　　　　　　　　minimum 45 m

Status
In service with the Soviet Navy and the navies of Egypt and other Arab nations.

(USSR)

SA-NX-6

This high-performance surface-to-air missile first went to sea aboard the *Kara* class cruiser *Azov*, but this may have been a trials installation. *Kirov* class battlecruisers have 12 launch silos for this vertical-launch missile which may be a navalised version of the land-based SA-10 system. The associated radar is the Top Dome. The weapon is also expected to arm a new class of guided-missile cruiser, the prototype of which was under construction at a Black Sea shipyard in 1981.

(USSR)

SA-N-?

A new medium range surface-to-air missile system is reported to have been deployed aboard the cruiser *Sovremenny*, but this has not yet been confirmed. If the SA-N-3 Goblet is a navalisation of the land-based SA-6 Gainful, the new system may be a naval version of the SA-11.

ORDNANCE

TWIN 3-inch MOUNTING

(CANADA)

Some frigates of the Canadian fleet are fitted with twin 76 mm AA mountings of Canadian manufacture. In the *Mackenzie* class there is a 70-calibre Canadian twin forward and a 50-calibre twin of US manufacture aft: in the *Restigouche* class there is either a similar arrangement or just the 70-calibre Canadian twin.

Performance details are assumed to be similar to the UK (Vickers) Mk 6 70-calibre twin 76 mm weapon.

Status
Operational as stated.

HMCS *Saskatchewan* with twin 3-inch mounting.

(CHINA)

Twin 130 mm mountings are being incorporated in the new *Luta* class destroyers of the Chinese (PRC) Navy. Externally they look very much like the elderly Russian weapons of the same calibre; but it is reasonable to assume that the design will have been modernised in details.

Gun data are assumed to be broadly similar to those of the Russian weapon; but again it may be assumed that performance will have been upgraded to some extent.

TWIN AND SINGLE 130 mm MOUNTINGS

Single Mountings
Single mountings of what is probably the same gun have been installed during refit in several of the old naval vessels inherited by the PRC from their predecessors.

Status
Operational in new destroyers and old escorts.

(CHINA)

Twin and single dual-purpose guns of Chinese manufacture have been installed in some of the refitted escorts of the miscellaneous fleet inherited by the PRC from their predecessors.

No details of construction or performance are available but the weapons are assumed to be broadly similar to the more modern 100 mm Russian weapons on which the Chinese designs are probably based.

TWIN AND SINGLE 100 mm MOUNTINGS

Status
Operational in older vessels of the Chinese Navy.

(CHINA)

Twin 57 mm dual-purpose mountings are installed in the new *Luta* class destroyers of the Chinese (PRC) Navy. No details of construction or performance are available, but it is reasonable to assume that the designs of both gun and mounting are based on Russian designs — but probably not the latest Russian design since this entered service after the estrangement between the two countries.

TWIN 57 mm MOUNTING

Status
Operational in new destroyers of the Chinese Navy.

(CHINA)

Twin 37 mm AA mountings which are fairly certainly made in China are installed in several of the light craft built in Chinese yards in recent years.

No details of construction or performance are available but the weapons are apparently copies of the side-by-side twin 37 mm Russian mountings and are probably essentially similar in performance.

TWIN 37 mm MOUNTING

Status
Operational in modern light vessels of the Chinese Navy.

(CHINA)

Twin 25 mm AA mountings are installed in various light craft of the Chinese (PRC) Navy. Many of these weapons were undoubtedly made in Russia and are of the same designs as those installed in similar vessels in that country; it is believed, however, that new weapons are being built in China — presumably to similar standards.

TWIN 25 mm MOUNTING

Status
Operational.

TWIN 5-inch MOUNTING

Although this 127 mm gun is of French design and manufacture it was designed to use standard American 5-inch gun ammunition, and for that reason it has here been described by its Imperial measure calibre.

Now fitted only in the Type T53 destroyers *Forbin* and *Tartu*, these dual-purpose guns have elsewhere been replaced by the new single 100 mm gun. The twin-gun turret weighs about 45 tons.

Gun Data
Calibre: 127 mm (5-inch)
Barrel length: 54 calibres
Elevation: to 80°
Projectile weight: 32 kg
Muzzle velocity: 850 m/sec
Rate of fire: 15 rounds/barrel/min
Maximum range: 22 km (12 nm)
Maximum altitude: 13,000 m
Date introduced: 1953

Status
Operational as stated above.

Forbin destroyer of the French Navy. Forward gun is twin 5-inch mounting.

Considered by the French Navy to be of the optimum calibre for engaging air and surface targets, this fully-automatic gun is now that service's standard armament. It is installed on most of the larger new and refitted vessels. Current version is the Model 1968-II which has succeeded the earlier Models 64 and 68-I.

Gun Data
Calibre: 100 mm
Barrel length: 55 calibres
Elevation: –15 to +80°
Projectile weight: 13.5 kg (complete round 23.2 kg)
Muzzle velocity: 870 m/sec
Rate of fire: 60 rounds/min
Maximum range: 17 km (9 nm)
Mounting weight: 24.5 tons
Date introduced: 1960

Manufacturer
Creusot-Loire turret; CSEE (control gear), design by Direction Technique de Constructions Navales (DTCN)

Status
Operational with the French Navy and with the navies of Argentina, Belgium, Germany, Greece and Portugal.

100 mm COMPACT
Creusot is developing a lightweight 100 mm gun mounting based on the standard French Navy version. This will weigh only 17 tons and have a rate of fire which can be varied from 10 to 90 rounds/min.

The *Commandant Rivière*. Forward gun is single 100 mm mounting.

TWIN 57 mm MOUNTING

(FRANCE)

This 57 mm AA weapon is still in widespread French Navy service, although no longer being fitted to new vessels. Consisting of two Bofors guns on a mount of French design, it carries an ammunition reserve of 80 rounds per gun. The 16 ton mounting is normally operated by remote control.

Gun Data
Calibre: 57 mm
Barrel length: 60 calibres
Elevation: –8 to +93°
Projectile weight: 2.96 kg
Muzzle velocity: 865 m/sec
Rate of fire: 120 rounds/barrel/min
Maximum range: 13 km (7 nm)
Mounting weight: 16 tons
Date introduced: 1950

Manufacturer
Direction Technique de Constructions Navales (DTCN)

Status
In service with the French Navy.

SINGLE 30 mm REMOTE-CONTROLLED MOUNTING

(FRANCE)

This French-designed mounting incorporates the Oerlikon (formerly Hispano-Suiza) HSS 831A gun and is a remotely-controlled turret mount which can be operated from an external aiming post or aimed by one or two gun layers. Primarily an anti-aircraft mounting it can be used to engage surface targets. 215 rounds are carried on a belt feed on the mounting which weighs 3.6 tons.

Gun Data
Calibre: 30 mm
Barrel length: 70 calibres
Elevation: –18 to +83°
Traverse: 350°
Elevation speed: 40°/sec
Traverse speed: 50°/sec
Projectile weight: 0.42 kg
Muzzle velocity: 1,000 m/sec
Rate of fire: 600 rounds/min
Tactical range: 2,800 m (maximum 10 km [5.4 nm])

Manufacturer
Mounting: S.A.A.M. Gun: Oerlikon-Bührle

Status
Operational.

Twin 57 mm mounting aboard L'Alsacien, type E-52 frigate of the French Navy.

(FRANCE)

Numerous mountings of Hispano 30 mm guns are to be found in the French Navy, as in many others, on a variety of ships. Performances of such weapons differ in detail from the figures given on page 62 but the broad picture is similar.

(FRANCE)

DTCN is studying a naval mounting for the F2 20 mm automatic cannon. Designed for one-man operation, this would have manually powered traverse and elevation, with a total of 300 rounds being carried on the mount.

(WEST GERMANY)

This is a naval version of the widely-used Rheinmetall Mk 20 rapid-fire gun, a lightweight manually directed weapon.

(ISRAEL)

This air-defence weapon consists of two HSS 831 30 mm cannon on an electrically-driven turret, which contains rate gyros to stabilise the barrels against the ship's motion. Each cannon has a 125-round ammunition feed box on the mounting, and these are connected to the breeches via a semi-rigid guideway.

OLDER 30 mm MOUNTINGS

20 mm TYPE A NAVAL MOUNTING

Gun Data
Calibre: 20 mm
Elevation: −15 to +60°
Projectile weight: 90 or 120 grammes
Muzzle velocity: 1,050 or 1,300 m/sec
Rate of fire: 740 rounds/min
Maximum range: 1.2-2 km
Mounting weight: 0.47 tons

Manufacturer
DTCN

20 mm MARK 20 Rh202

Gun Data
Calibre: 20 mm
Elevation: −10 to +60°
Muzzle velocity: 1,050-1,150 m/sec
Rate of fire: 1,000 rounds/min (may be reduced to 600 rounds/min if required)
Maximum range: 2 km
Mounting weight: 0.4 tons

Manufacturer
Rheinmetall

Status
In production; in service with several navies.

TCM 30 TWIN MOUNTING

Gun Data
Calibre: 30 mm
Elevation: −20 to +85°
Muzzle velocity: 1,080 m/sec
Rate of fire: 650 rounds/barrel/min

Manufacturer
Israel Aircraft Industries

20 mm Mark 20 RU 202

This is a dual-purpose gun mount intended as a main armament for frigates and destroyers.

Ready-use ammunition is held in three drums just below the turret. A central elevator hoists the ammunition, chosen from one drum, and delivers it to the turret where two oscillating arms perform the final movement to the loading trays.

The drums are automatically reloaded through two hoists manually loaded in the magazine. The layout permits storage of three different types of ammunition in the ready-use magazine. Remote-controlled fuse setters are provided in the oscillating arms.

The reloading, feeding, loading and firing sequence is controlled by a control console operated by a single man. Optionally, the mount can also be fitted with a stabilised line-of-sight local control system.

The barrel is fitted with a multi-muzzle brake. The shield is of glass-fibre and is watertight. The complete mounting weighs 54 tons.

Gun Data
Calibre: 127 mm
Barrel length: 54 calibres
Elevation: − 15 to +85°
Traverse: 350°
Elevation speed: 30°/sec
Traverse speed: 40°/sec
Projectile weight: probably about 32 kg
Muzzle velocity: probably about 850 m/sec
Rate of fire: 45 rounds/min
Ready-use ammunition: 69 rounds
Maximum range: probably about 22 km (12 nm)
Date introduced: 1969

Manufacturer
OTO Melara

Status
In service with the Italian Navy and ordered or in service with the navies of Canada, Egypt, Nigeria and Peru.

Single 127/54 gun mounting.

The 76/62 OTO M.M.I. single barrel automatic gun was developed as secondary armament for frigates and corvettes as a dual-purpose weapon system.

The gun is a single barrel, water-spray cooled, on a powered mounting. It is protected by a watertight splinterproof shield, which also houses the one man required to direct the gun.

The feed system can vary in length from a minimum of 2.5 m to a maximum of 11 m from loading tray to magazine. Ammunition is fixed and empty cases ejected automatically. Three men are required to reload the ammunition system.

Elevation and traverse are electrically and hydraulically controlled and there is provision for emergency manual operation. Either local or remote control is possible. The complete mounting weights about 12 tons.

Gun Data

Calibre: 76 mm
Barrel length: 62 calibres
Elevation: –15 to +85°
Traverse: 360°
Elevation speed: 40°/sec
Traverse speed: 70°/sec
Projectile weight: approx 6 kg
Muzzle velocity: approx 900 m/sec
Rate of fire: 60 rounds/min
Maximum range: approx 16 km (8.5 nm)
Date introduced: 1962

Manufacturer

OTO Melara

Status

In service in many Italian ships. No longer in production and superseded by the 76/62 Compact.

Single 76/72 mm mounting.

SINGLE 76/62 COMPACT MOUNTING

Developed from the 76/62 M.M.I. mounting this fully-automatic OTO mount is designed for dual-purpose use on ships of any type from hydrofoils and motor gunboats upwards.

The ammunition system is designed to sustain a high rate of fire. Rounds are hoisted from the magazine in a series of short movements to reduce acceleration forces on moving parts and on the ammunition.

Primarily the mount is designed for remote control but there is emergency local control and a stabilised line-of-sight local control system can be fitted. Normal control is electrical.

The gun is fitted with a small-hole muzzle brake and fume extractor; the gunhouse shield is made of glass-fibre and the complete mounting weighs 7.5 tons.

Gun Data
Calibre: 76 mm
Barrel length: 62 calibres
Elevation: –15 to +85°
Traverse: unlimited
Elevation speed: 35°/sec
Traverse speed: 60°/sec
Projectile weight: 6.2 kg
Muzzle velocity: 925 m/sec
Rate of fire: 85 rounds/min
Maximum range: approx 16 km (9 nm)
Maximum altitude: approx 11,500 m
Date introduced: 1969

Manufacturer
OTO Melara

Status
Manufactured in Italy, the United States (as the 76 mm 62-calibre Gun Mount Mk 75), and Japan as well as being in partial production in Spain. Operational on a wide range of vessels.

Single 76/62 Compact mounting.

(ITALY)

The Breda Compact Twin 40 mm 70-calibre naval mounting is particularly intended for point defence against aircraft or anti-ship missiles. It is fully automatic and uses high performance remote-controlled servo systems which, with low-inertia design of the gun mounting arrangements, gives the weapon a high-quality mechanical performance.

Two versions of the mounting provide alternatives of 736 or 444 rounds in the magazine. Normally the magazine will be mounted below deck but it is sufficiently compact for an above deck mounting to be constructed if necessary. In their normal configuration the two alternative mounts weigh 5,200 kg (Type A) plus 1,800 kg for 736 rounds or 4,900 kg (Type B) plus 1,100 kg for 444 rounds.

Gun characteristics are generally similar to the Bofors L/70 except that angular velocities are 90°/sec in both angles and accelerations are 120°/sec/sec. The weapon is used in the Dardo point-defence system.

COMPACT TWIN 40/70 MOUNTING

Gun Data
Calibre: 40 mm
Barrel length: 70 calibres
Elevation: –13 to +85°
Muzzle velocity: 1,000 m/sec
Rate of fire: 300 rounds/barrel/min

Manufacturer
Breda Meccanica Bresciana

Status
Entering service with a number of navies.

Compact Twin 40/70 mounting aboard Peruvian *Lupo* class frigate, *Carvajal*.

Bofors 40 mm and 70-calibre guns, like their 60-calibre predecessors, are made or adapted under licence in many countries. In particular, a series of variants on the basic mounting has been engineered by Breda Meccanica Bresciana, in Italy, with special reference to automatic feed systems. Except that the loading system clearly influences the capacity of the installation for sustained fire, the basic characteristics of the gun are unaltered in these different configurations: visually, however, the mountings are very different and some of them are illustrated here.

Status
Like the basic gun the Breda variants are in widespread service use.

TWIN MOUNTING
TYPE 106
Special Characteristics
Magazine capacity: 32 rounds/barrel
Weight: 6,510 kg without ammunition plus 100 kg for battery
Angular speeds: 95°/sec
Angular accelerations: 125°/sec/sec

TYPE 64
Special Characteristics
Magazine capacity: 100 rounds/barrel
Control: local or remote
Weight: 7,900 kg without ammunition plus 150 kg for battery
Elevation speed: 95°/sec
Traverse speed: 85°/sec
Elevation acceleration: 125°/sec/sec
Traverse acceleration: 110°/sec/sec

SINGLE MOUNTING
TYPE 107
Special Characteristics
Magazine capacity: 32 rounds
Control: local or remote
Weight: 3,610 kg without ammunition plus 100 kg for battery
Angular speeds: 95°/sec
Angular accelerations: 125°/sec/sec

Status
In production and service.

TYPE 564
Special Characteristics
Magazine capacity: 144 rounds
Control: local or remote
Weight: 3,300 kg without ammunition plus 100 kg for battery
Crew: normally 2 on the mount with a third at standby. A version requiring only 1 on the mount is available
Elevation speed: 45°/sec
Traverse speed: 80°/sec
Elevation acceleration: 130°/sec/sec
Traverse acceleration: 120°/sec/sec

Breda/Bofors 40 mm Type 564.

TWIN 35 mm OE/OTO GUN MOUNTING

The 35 mm OE/OTO mounting has been produced as a private venture and is intended for use in any type of ship. It is primarily for close anti-aircraft defence, with a secondary anti-ship and anti-shore role.

Two types of turret have been designed, the first for installation above the weather deck; and the second for installation with the shank below deck level. For each type there are two fire-control systems — remote control and local control with sight for optical tracking.

The Oerlikon KDA gun has a high rate of fire and is belt fed. An interesting feature is that two belts are fed to each gun, and either may be selected in about two seconds. Thus the mounting can switch very rapidly from firing, say, anti-aircraft ammunition to armour-piercing. Each gun is provided with EVA at the muzzle to measure muzzle velocity, and this information is fed back into the computer to permit corrections in laying to be applied.

Gun Data
Calibre: 35 mm
Barrel length: 90 calibres
Elevation: −15 to +85°
Traverse: unlimited
Elevation speed: maximum 75°/sec
Traverse speed: maximum 115°/sec
Elevation acceleration: 140°/sec/sec
Traverse acceleration: 130°/sec/sec
Crew: 3 (2 loaders, 1 layer, if not remotely controlled)
Muzzle velocity: 1,175 m/sec
Rate of fire: 550 rounds/barrel/min
Maximum range: 6 km (3 nm)
Maximum altitude: 5,000 m
Date introduced: 1972 (gun)

Manufacturer
OTO Melara

Status
In production for Libyan 550 ton corvettes.

OE/OTO 35 mm naval twin mount.

Prototype EX-83 gun for the Goalkeeper, close-in ship defence system.

GOALKEEPER

By combining the General Electric EX-83 mounting with new surveillance and tracking radars developed by Hollandse Signaalapparaten, the Royal Netherlands Navy hopes to arm its *Standard* class frigates with a weapon capable of destroying sea-skimming anti-ship missiles. Prototypes are due to be delivered by early 1983 and the weapon is due to be deployed around 1985. The EX-83 mount — which is also being tested by the US Navy coupled with a Lockheed Mk 86 fire-control system — carries the seven-barrelled GAU-8/A 30 mm cannon originally developed for the US Air Force but the discarding-sabot ammunition used will have a penetrator made from tungsten rather than the depleted uranium used by the US services.

Gun Data
Calibre: 30 mm
Barrel length: 96 calibres
Elevation: –25 to +83°
Projectile weight: approx 0.4 kg
Muzzle velocity: 1,030 m/sec
Rate of fire: 2,100-4,200 rounds/min
Mounting weight: approx 4 tons

Manufacturer
Mounting and gun: General Electric
Radars: Hollandse Signaalapparaten

Status
Under development for the Royal Netherlands Navy.

SINGLE 3-inch 50-CALIBRE MOUNTING MARK 34

This is an American designed weapon built in Spain and mounted on destroyers and frigates of the Spanish Navy. Details of this mounting and of the American designed and built twin Mk 33 mountings, which are also mounted on Spanish destroyers and frigates, will be found in the US entries below, but the main data for the Mk 34 are recapitulated here.

Gun Data
Calibre: 76 mm (3-inch)
Barrel length: 50 calibres
Elevation: to 85°
Projectile weight: approx 6 kg
Muzzle velocity: approx 825 m/sec
Rate of fire: 50 rounds/min
Maximum range: approx 13 km (7 nm)

Manufacturer
Fabrica de Artilleria, Sociedad Española de construccion Naval

Status
Operational.

SINGLE 40 mm 70-CALIBRE MOUNTING

This version of the Bofors L/70 40 mm AA gun is built under licence in Spain and installed in Spanish warships. The mounting weighs 2.5 tons.

Gun Data
Calibre: 40 mm
Barrel length: 70 calibres
Elevation: –10 to +90°
Elevation speed: 45°/sec
Traverse: 85°/sec unlimited
Projectile weight: 0.95 kg
Muzzle velocity: approx 1,000 m/sec
Rate of fire: 240 rounds/min
Tactical range: 4,000 m (maximum 12 km [6.5 nm])

Manufacturer
Empresa Nacional Bazan

Status
Operational.

(SPAIN)

Similar in concept to the US Vulcan/Phalanx system, Meroka uses an array of 12 fixed gun barrels rather than a Gatling arrangement to obtain the required rate of fire. The guns are based on the Oerlikon GA1-B01 and the barrels are mounted in two rows of six. Initial aiming is by means of an optical gyro gunsight, with a Lockheed Electronics Doppler radar being used for tracking purposes.

Twenty systems are currently on order to equip a range of Spanish Navy vessels including the FFG-7 frigates and the aircraft carrier *Dedalo*.

MEROKA NAVAL AIR DEFENCE SYSTEM

Gun Data
Calibre: 20 mm
Barrel length: 120 calibres
Rate of fire: 2,700-3,600 rounds/min
Maximum range: over 2 km (1 nm)

Manufacturer
Empresa Nacional Bazan

Status
Under development for the Spanish Navy.

Meroka naval air defence system.

(SWEDEN)

These 6-inch (152 mm) Bofors guns were first introduced in 1942 and are now to be found as a triple mounting only in the cruiser *Latorre* of the Chilean Navy (formerly the *Göta Lejon* of the Royal Swedish Navy).

Twin and Single Mountings
The same guns are also installed in twin mountings in the *Latorre* and in the cruisers *Almirante Grau* of the Peruvian Navy and *De Zeven Provincien* of the Royal Netherlands Navy. The single 6-inch guns of the minelayer *Alvsnabben* of the Royal Swedish Navy are believed to be of the same pattern.

TRIPLE 6-inch MOUNTING

Gun Data
Calibre: 152 mm (6-inch)
Barrel length: 53 calibres
Elevation: 60°
Projectile weight: 46 kg
Muzzle velocity: 900 m/sec
Rate of fire: 10 rounds/barrel/min
Maximum range: 26 km (14 nm)
Date introduced: 1942

Manufacturer
Bofors

Status
Operational but no longer manufactured.

(SWEDEN)

These 50-calibre Bofors 120 mm guns are mounted in twin mounts on the *Halland* class destroyers of the Royal Swedish Navy, on the *Tromp*, *Halland* and *Friesland* class anti-submarine escorts of the Royal Netherlands Navy, one *Halland* class destroyer of the Peruvian Navy and on modified *Halland* class destroyers of the Colombian Navy. They are fully automatic and radar controlled and the complete twin mounting weighs 67 tons.

Left: Bofors triple 6-inch gun mounting.

Below: Twin 120 mm automatic mounting on *Halland* class destroyer of the Royal Netherlands Navy.

TWIN 120 mm AUTOMATIC MOUNTING

Gun Data
Calibre: 120 mm
Barrel length: 50 calibres
Elevation: to 85°
Projectile weight: 23.5 kg
Muzzle velocity: 850 m/sec
Rate of fire: 40 rounds/barrel/min
Maximum range: 20.5 km (11 nm)
Maximum altitude: 12,500 m
Date introduced: 1950

Manufacturer
AB Bofors

Status
Operational as stated.

SINGLE 120/46 AUTOMATIC MOUNTING

(SWEDEN)

The Bofors L/46 120 mm Automatic Gun is designed for use against both surface and airborne targets and has a very high rate of fire.

Housed in a 4 mm steel turret mount the gun has two magazines, mounted on the elevating cradle, which are manually filled from a fixed-structure motor-driven rod hoist. Electro-hydraulic remote control is standard with the alternative of gyro-stabilised one-man local control. Telescopic sights are also fitted and the hoist and the elevation and traverse mechanisms can be operated by hand. The gun barrel is liquid cooled and has an exchangeable liner. The complete mounting (less ammunition) weighs 28.5 tons. 52 rounds are carried in the magazine.

Gun Data
Calibre: 120 mm
Barrel length: 46 calibres
Elevation: –10 to +80°
Projectile weight: 21 kg (round 35 kg)
Muzzle velocity: 1,800 m/sec
Rate of fire: 80 rounds/min
Maximum range: 18.5 km (10 nm)
Maximum altitude: 11,800 m
Date introduced: 1967

Manufacturer
AB Bofors

Status
In service aboard frigates of the Finnish and Indonesian Navies.

Single 120/46 automatic mounting.

SINGLE 3-inch AUTOMATIC MOUNTING

(SWEDEN)

This is a sturdy, simple, remotely-controlled single gun designed for surface fire. Weighing only 6,500 kg and requiring only two loaders in the ammunition room, it is suitable for installation in small ships and is currently in service on *Storm* class fast patrol boats of the Norwegian Navy.

Electro-hydraulic remote control is used. The gun is mounted in a 6 mm steel gun house and has a fixed motor-driven hoist with lifting link levers and 5-round feed device. 100 rounds are carried in the magazine and hoist. The gun has a monobloc barrel.

Gun Data
Calibre: 76 mm (3-inch)
Barrel length: 50 calibres
Elevation: –10 to +30°
Projectile weight: 5.9 kg (round 11 kg)
Muzzle velocity: 825 m/sec
Rate of fire: 30 rounds/min
Maximum range: 12.6 km (7 nm)
Date introduced: 1965

Manufacturer
AB Bofors

Status
No longer in production. Designed and developed as a private venture by Bofors, this gun was first conceived in 1962 and went into service with the Norwegian Navy in 1965.

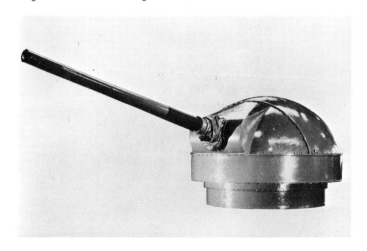

Single 3-inch automatic mounting.

Introduced in 1950, these 60-calibre guns were at one time widely fitted. Now, however, they are to be found in the cruiser *Latorre* (formerly *Göta Lejon*) of the Chilean Navy and the *Halland* class destroyers of the Royal Swedish Navy. The same gun in a slightly different twin mounting is still in service in the French Navy.

The complete turret of the Swedish installations weighs some 24 tons.

Gun Data

Calibre: 57 mm
Barrel length: 60 calibres
Elevation: –10 to +90°
Projectile weight: 2.6 kg
Muzzle velocity: 900 m/sec
Rate of fire: 130 rounds/barrel/min
Maximum range: 14.5 km (7.8 nm)
Maximum altitude: 10,300 m
Date introduced: 1950

Manufacturer
AB Bofors

Status
Operational but no longer in production.

Twin 57 mm gun mounting.

SINGLE 57 mm L/70 AUTOMATIC MOUNTING

(SWEDEN)

This 57 mm Bofors single gun in a plastic gun house is designed for both surface and anti-aircraft fire.

Alternatives of electro-hydraulic remote control or gyro-stabilised one-man local control are available. The gunfeed system contains 40 rounds of ready-use ammunition, with 128 rounds stowed in racks within the gunhouse, and there are dual step-by-step fixed supply hoists. The barrel is liquid-cooled.

Two types of ammunition are available: one is a proximity-fused and pre-fragmented shell for use against aerial targets; the other is a special surface target shell which penetrates the target and is detonated after a short delay.

The gun can be equipped with rocket-launching rails for 2-inch (51 mm) rockets.

A new Mk 2 version with a smaller turret and fully automatic reloading system is expected to be available during 1981.

Gun Data
Calibre: 57 mm
Barrel length: 70 calibres
Elevation: −10 to +75°
Projectile weight: 2.4 kg (round 5.9 kg)
Muzzle velocity: 1,025 m/sec
Rate of fire: 200 rounds/min
Maximum range: 14 km (7.5 nm)
Date introduced: 1971

Manufacturer
AB Bofors

Status
Operational with the Swedish Navy (*Spica* and *Hugin* fast-attack craft). Ordered by the Norwegian Navy for Coast Guard use.

Single 57 mm L/70 automatic mounting on *Spica T131* class fast-attack craft of the Royal Swedish Navy.

Bofors make a number of different mountings for their 40 mm 70-calibre naval guns, which can be used against both surface and aerial targets.

Current models have electro-hydraulic laying equipment and can be fitted for remote or local control. In local control such guns are gyro-stabilised and have reflex sights with speed rings for aiming. There are also unpowered mounts.

Manually loaded guns are made with open mountings or equipped with a light plastic cupola for weather protection. Automatically loaded guns are also made using automatic feed devices built by Breda.

Gun Data
Calibre: 40 mm
Barrel length: 70 calibres
Elevation: –10 to +90°
Traverse: unlimited
Elevation speed: 45°/sec (powered mounts)
Traverse speed: 85°/sec (powered mounts)
Projectile weight: 0.96 kg HE (round 2.4 kg)
Muzzle velocity: approx 1,000 m/sec
Rate of fire: 300 rounds/min
Tactical range: 4,000 m (maximum approx 12 km [6.5 nm])
Mount weight: (single mounts) 2.8-3.3 tons according to type
Date introduced: 1946 but continuously improved. Current basic design dates from late 1950s

Manufacturer
In Sweden, AB Bofors

Status
In widespread service in the Royal Swedish Navy and many others.

40 mm 70-calibre mountings on *Hano* class coastal mine-sweeper of the Royal Swedish Navy.

Single 40/60 mounting.

SINGLE 40/60 MOUNTING

This 60-calibre version of the well-known Bofors 40 mm AA gun was introduced in 1942 and is still in service in many places. Its performance is, as one would expect, somewhat inferior to that of the modern 70-calibre weapon.

Gun Data
Calibre: 40 mm
Barrel length: 60 calibres
Elevation: to 80°
Projectile weight: 0.9 kg
Muzzle velocity: 830 m/sec
Rate of fire: 120 rounds/min
Maximum range: 10 km (5.4 nm)
Tactical range: 3 km (1.6 nm)
Maximum altitude: 5,600 m
Date introduced: 1942

Manufacturer
AB Bofors

Status
In service and still fitted in reconditioned form but obsolescent and no longer in production.

(SWITZERLAND)

TWIN 35 mm MOUNTING TYPE GDM-A

Type GDM-A is an electrically-controlled, stabilised twin gun that can function either with radar fire-control equipment or with an optical director equipment with auxiliary computer. In addition the gun is equipped with locally stabilised column control and a gunsight. The gun can also be controlled manually by handwheel.

The two weapons are completely interchangeable and can be assembled for left or right feed. The hand cocking devices and barrels belonging to each weapon are also completely interchangeable.

Gun Data
Calibre: 35 mm
Barrel length: 90 calibres
Elevation: –15 to +85°
Muzzle velocity: 1,175 m/sec
Rate of fire: 550 rounds/barrel/min
Date introduced: 1972

Manufacturer
Oerlikon-Bührle

Status
In service with the navies of Ecuador, Greece, Iran, Libya and Ghana.

Twin 35 mm mounting type GDM-A.

TWIN 30 mm GUN MOUNTING GCM-A

This twin 30 mm gun is intended to arm small vessels such as fast-attack craft and uses a gyro-stabilised gun to counter the effects of ship movement. It may also be fitted to larger vessels for point defence. Target tracking is via a Ferranti gyro-stabilised sight, but the weapon can also be directed by radar. A total of 320 ready-use rounds are carried to feed the twin KCB cannon.

Gun Data
Calibre: 30 mm
Barrel length: 75 calibres
Elevation: –15 to +80°
Muzzle velocity: 1,080 m/sec
Rate of fire: 650 rounds/barrel/min

Manufacturer
Oerlikon-Bührle

20 mm MOUNTING TYPE GAM/B01

This is a simple, but modern and efficient, 20 mm naval mounting embodying the KAA cannon.

All-up weight is low enough to permit installation on any type of naval vessel and the gun can be used for either AA or surface fire. No electrical power is needed: the gun is laid by the gunner using a shoulder-harness and sighting is by simple ring and bead.

Similar weapons are also produced in 25 mm (GBM/A01) and with an alternative KAD cannon (GAM/C01).

EARLIER MODELS
Very large numbers of manually-operated single 20 mm cannon of earlier types are to be found in very many navies. The modern weapon described above is typical of current practice: the earlier weapons are too numerous to list but it may be assumed that their performance is generally inferior to that of the GAM/B01.

Gun Data
Calibre: 20 mm
Elevation: –15 to +60°
Muzzle velocity: 1,050 m/sec
Rate of fire: maximum 1,200 rounds/min
Ready Rounds: 200
Feed system: link belt

Manufacturer
Oerlikon-Bührle

Status
In service with the Spanish and other navies.

20 mm mounting Type GAM/B01.

Many older patterns of single 20 mm remain in service.

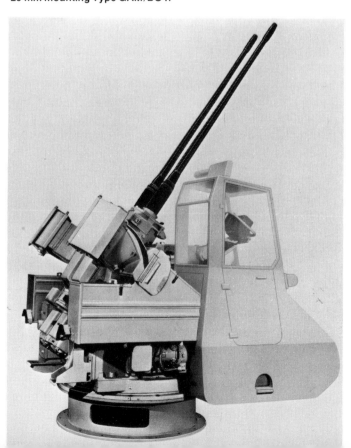

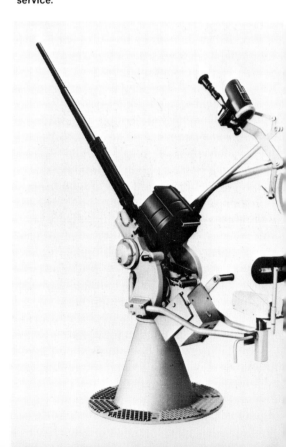

(SWITZERLAND)

This widely used Oerlikon mounting incorporates the Type 804 drum-fed cannon. Suitable for small and very small naval vessels it is operated entirely by one man and can be used for either AA or surface fire. Sighting is by ring and bead. The complete mount weighs 240 kg.

20 mm MOUNTING TYPE A41/804

Gun Data
Calibre: 20 mm
Muzzle velocity: 835 m/sec
Rate of fire: 800 rounds/min
Ready rounds: 60 in drum magazine

Manufacturer
Oerlikon-Bührle

Status
Weapon operational but no longer made.

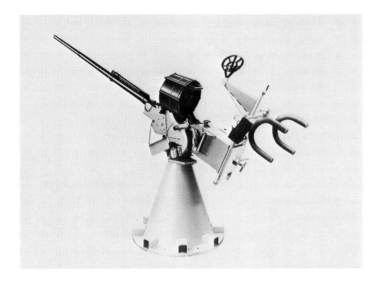

20 mm mounting Type A41/804.

(UK/INDIA)

This 1934 pattern Vickers gun is no longer in service with the Royal Navy, though the guns may be seen on the cruiser *Belfast* now preserved as a floating museum in London. The triple 6-inch gun mounting on the Indian cruiser *Mysore* (formerly HMS *Nigeria*) is, however, believed to use the 1934 gun. The mounting weighs about 135 tons but can be traversed by hand if power fails.

TRIPLE 6-inch GUN MOUNTING

Gun Data
Calibre: 152 mm (6-inch)
Barrel length: 50 calibres
Elevation: to 45°
Traverse: 240° total
Projectile weight: 50 kg
Muzzle velocity: 820 m/sec
Rate of fire: 8 rounds/barrel/min
Maximum range: 23 km (12 nm)
Date introduced: 1934

Manufacturer
Vickers

Status
Believed to be in service in only one ship.

Triple 6-inch gun mounting aboard HMS *Belfast*.

TWIN 6-inch MOUNTING MARK 26

This twin automatic dual-purpose mount is remotely radar-controlled and electrically traversed and elevated. It is also fitted with local sighting equipment and joystick control. It is notable for the high rate of fire that can be achieved. Weight of the twin-gun turret is about 163 tons and the gun crew number 16.

Gun Data
Calibre: 152 mm (6-inch)
Elevation: to 80°
Rate of fire: 20 rounds/barrel/min
Date introduced: 1951

Manufacturer
Vickers

Status
Fitted to the *Tiger* class cruisers now being retired from active Royal Navy service.

Twin 6-inch mounting Mk 26 aboard HMS *Tiger*.

(UK)

This twin-barrelled remotely-controlled power-operated mounting is in operational use in many ships of the Royal Navy and others. Normally remotely-controlled electro-hydraulically it can also be controlled locally by a joystick. The loading cycle is semi-automatic, shell and cartridge being separately hoisted and manually loaded into the loading tray. The turret weighs about 50 tons.

TWIN 4.5-inch MOUNTING MARK 6

Gun Data
Calibre: 114 mm (4.5-inch)
Barrel length: approx 50 calibres
Elevation: to approx 80°
Projectile weight: approx 25 kg
Muzzle velocity: approx 850 m/sec
Rate of fire: 20 rounds/barrel/min
Maximum range: approx 19 km (10 nm)
Date introduced: 1946

Manufacturer
Vickers

Status
In widespread operational use.

Twin 4.5-inch mounting Mk 6 aboard HMS *Antrim*.

(UK)

This single mounting is to be found in the *Tribal* class frigates of the Royal Navy and in similar vessels elsewhere. It is manually loaded and normally remotely-controlled but can be controlled locally by joystick. Charge and shell are separate and automatically rammed.

SINGLE 4.5-inch MOUNTING MARK 5

Gun Data
Calibre: 114 mm (4.5-inch)
Barrel length: 45 calibres
Elevation: to approx 50°
Projectile weight: approx 25 kg
Muzzle velocity: approx 840 m/sec
Rate of fire: up to 14 rounds/min
Maximum range: approx 19 km (10 nm)
Date introduced: 1937

Manufacturer
Vickers

Status
Operational as noted but no longer made. The *Tribal* class is about to be retired.

Single 4.5-inch mounting Mk 5 on HMS *Ashanti*.

SINGLE 4.5-inch MOUNTING MARK 8

This fully-automatic gun is modelled on the British Army's Abbot gun and is fitted with muzzle brake and fume extractor. A completely new range of fixed ammunition has also been designed.

Major features of design of the mounting are a simple ammunition feed system and a remote power control system with large stability margins. The revolving structure has been kept light and a sandwich-construction glass-reinforced plastic gun-shield fitted.

The loading system is hydraulically operated and employs only four transfer points between the gun bay (ready-use magazine) and the gun, and the type of ammunition may be changed without unloading or firing out a large number of rounds. A stockpile of ammunition may be accommodated at the mounting and fired remotely from the Operations Room with no crew closed up at the mounting.

Single 4.5-inch mounting Mk 8 on HMS _Sheffield_, Type 42 destroyer.

Gun Data
Calibre: 114 mm (4.5-inch)
Barrel length: 55 calibres
Elevation: −10 to +55°
Muzzle velocity: 850 m/sec
Rate of fire: 20 rounds/min
Maximum range: 22 km (12 nm)
Date introduced: 1971

Manufacturer
Vickers

Status
Operational with the Royal Navy (Type 82 and Type 42 destroyers, Type 21 frigates), Argentine Navy (Type 42 destroyers), Brazilian Navy (_Niteroi_ class frigates), Iran (_Saam_ class frigates), Libya (Mk 7 frigate) and Thailand (_Vosper_ frigate).

(UK)

105 mm AUTONOMOUS PATROL GUN

This mounting combines the well-proven Royal Ordnance Factories L7 105 mm tank gun with a fire-control system based on the Marconi Radar SFCS 600 system developed for tank use to produce a low-cost weapon for offshore patrol craft and similar vessels. The self-contained mounting is operated by a two-man crew and contains enough storage space for 30 rounds of ammunition. It is designed to be self-contained, requiring only external power, but can be linked to director control. For aiming purposes the turret is fitted with a day/night sight.

Gun Data
Calibre: 105 mm
Elevation: –12.5 to +55°
Rate of fire: 12-14 rounds/min
Mounting weight: 6 tons

Manufacturer
Royal Ordnance Factory Nottingham

(UK/CHILE)

SINGLE 4-inch MOUNTING

This fully-automatic 60-calibre weapon is mounted as four single mounts on the two *Almirante* class destroyers of the Chilean Navy.

Built by Vickers (as were the destroyers) and introduced in 1955, the gun and turret weigh a little over 26 tons.

Gun Data
Calibre: 102 mm (4-inch)
Barrel length: 60 calibres
Elevation: to 75°
Projectile weight: 16 kg
Muzzle velocity: 900 m/sec
Rate of fire: 40 rounds/min
Maximum range: 18.5 km (10 nm)
Maximum altitude: 12,000 m
Date introduced: 1955

Status
Operational but no longer in production.

Single 4-inch mounting on the *Almirante Riveros* of the Chilean Navy.

TWIN 3-inch MOUNTING MARK 6 (UK)

This is an automatic remotely-controlled electrically-driven mounting normally operated unmanned but with provision for local control. The turret weighs about 38 tons.

Gun Data
Calibre: 76 mm (3-inch)
Barrel length: 70 calibres
Elevation: to 80°
Projectile weight: probably about 7 kg
Muzzle velocity: probably about 1,000 m/sec
Rate of fire: 90 rounds/barrel/min
Maximum range: probably about 17 km (9 nm)
Date introduced: 1951

Manufacturer
Vickers

Status
Operational in British and Canadian warships.

TWIN 40 mm MOUNTING MARK 5 (UK)

A twin mounting of the Bofors 40/60 gun is in service in many British and Commonwealth naval vessels. Gun characteristics are the same as for the Swedish single 40/60 mounting and the twin mounting weighs approximately three tons. Single mounts are also in service.

The later Mk 7 British mounting uses the 40/70 Bofors gun.

30 mm LS30R GUN MOUNTING (UK)

Lawrence Scott & Electromotors has developed a lightweight power-driven and stabilised mounting for weapons such as the 30 mm RARDEN gun. The electronic and servo systems are similar to those used on the company's Optical Fire Director. The weapon is understood to be a private venture.

Gun Data
Calibre: 30 mm
Elevation: –20 to +70°
Muzzle velocity: 1,080-1,200 m/sec
Rate of fire: 90 rounds/min maximum (six-round burst)
Mounting weight: 0.8 tons

Manufacturer
Lawrence Scott & Electromotors

Twin 3-inch mounting Mk 6.

Twin 40 mm mounting Mk 5.

Mk 16 mounting on *Salem* class cruiser USS *Des Moines* now mothballed.

TRIPLE 16-inch GUN MOUNTING

(USA)

These 16-inch 50-calibre guns were the main armament of the *Iowa* class battleships of the US Navy. The individual guns weighed about 125 tons and the complete triple mounting some 2,000 tons. Bagged charges were used for the propellant of which 300 kg was used in six bags at a time.

Gun Data

Calibre: 406 mm (16-inch)
Barrel length: 50 calibres
Projectile weight: 935 kg
Muzzle velocity: 850 m/sec
Rate of fire: 2 rounds/barrel/min
Maximum range: 42 km (23 nm)
Date introduced: 1936

Status

The last of the *Iowa* class to be in service — and indeed the last battleship in the world to be in action — was the USS *New Jersey* whose guns are illustrated here. She was last decommissioned in December 1969 and placed in the Pacific reserve.

The US Government now plans to return the *New Jersey* to operational service after conversion to carry cruise missiles. This scheme will involve removing at least the aft-mounted 16-inch guns, but if the forward-mounted guns are retained, these veteran weapons will once again be in front-line US Navy service.

MARK 16 MOUNTING

(USA)

In the *Salem* class heavy cruisers of the US Navy an 8-inch 55-calibre gun designed to fire cased ammunition was installed in triple turrets. Apart from the modification to fire the new ammunition fully automatically the gun characteristics were generally similar to those of the earlier 8-inch semi-automatic guns. The turrets were larger, however, and the rate of fire was ten rounds per barrel per minute instead of five. The gun was first introduced in 1944.

Status

There were three heavy cruisers in the *Salem* class. The last of these to be in service was the *Newport News*, now in reserve.

Triple 16-inch guns of the battleship USS *New Jersey*.

Trials of this lightweight gun turret were carried out aboard the destroyer *Hull* between April 1974 and April 1975, but although these are reported to have gone well, the US Navy has decided to drop the weapon from its plans. The turret has been removed from the *Hull* and returned to the US Naval Surface Weapons Center for use as a test and demonstration mount.

The Mk 71 was intended to provide the US Navy with a weapon for ship-engagement and shore-bombardment, particularly since the heavy cruisers which had formerly discharged the latter task are now all in reserve. Progress with "smart" artillery rounds has now indicated that the required lethality may be obtained from existing calibres.

Gun Data
Calibre: 203 mm (8-inch)
Barrel length: 55 calibres
Projectile weight: 118 kg
Rate of fire: 12 rounds/min
Mounting weight: 78.4 tons

Manufacturer
Northern Ordnance Division, FMC

Status
Development project not adopted for service.

(USA)   TRIPLE 6-inch MARK 16 MOUNTING

This 6-inch 47-calibre gun mounting in a triple turret is of an old semi-automatic design but is still in service in a few light cruisers of the US Navy. The turrets are remotely-controlled but have local sighting and ranging facilities. The guns are independently laid and the turret weighs 154 tons.

Gun Data
Calibre: 152 mm (6-inch)
Barrel length: 47 calibres
Projectile weight: 46.5 kg
Muzzle velocity: approx 900 m/sec
Maximum range: approx 23.5 km (13 nm)
Date introduced: 1933

Status
These guns are believed to be in service on the ex-US Navy cruisers now serving in various South American navies.

A later version of this gun adapted to fire cased ammunition and to be used as a dual-purpose weapon was mounted in twin turrets on the large *Worcester* class light cruisers. The ships concerned have now been scrapped, however.

Single 8-inch lightweight gun mount Mk 71.

Triple 6-inch Mk 16 mounting on *Capitan Prat* of the Chilean Navy.

TWIN 5-inch 38-CALIBRE MARK 32 MOUNTING (USA)

This is the oldest design of 5-inch mounting still in service in the US Navy, but it is also one of the most widely used. The 5-inch 38-calibre gun has indeed been described as "the prototype of the conventional US naval gun".

The Mk 32 mounting contains two Mk 12 guns and an enclosed mounting with ammunition-handling room beneath. Remotely-controlled, semi-automatic, and dual-purpose it also has local laying facilities on the mounting. Fire angle limits are good but angular velocity and acceleration are significantly lower than those of the later 5-inch mountings.

Semi-fixed ammunition is used, consisting of a projectile weighing about 25 kg (varying according to type) and a case assembly weighing about 13 kg including a full powder charge of 6.8 kg. The ammunition is raised to the gun house by hydraulically powered hoists. The complete mounting weighs about 53 tons.

Gun Data

Calibre: 127 mm (5-inch)
Barrel length: 38 calibres
Elevation: –15 to +85°
Traverse: 300°
Projectile weight: approx 25 kg
Muzzle velocity: 792.5 m/sec maximum
Rate of fire: 15 rounds/barrel/min normal, 22 rounds/barrel/min emergency
Maximum range: 16.5 km (9 nm)
Maximum altitude: 11,000 m
Date introduced: 1935

Status

Twin mountings were installed in battleships, heavy cruisers and destroyers. Some of these are still in service in both the active and reserve fleets of the US Navy as well as in ex-US ships of other navies. They are also in service with Spanish-built ships of the Spanish Navy and some Italian-built destroyers.

SINGLE 5-inch 38-CALIBRE GUN MOUNTING (USA)

In addition to the enclosed twin mounting of the 5-inch 38-calibre gun there have been three other general types of mounting:

(a) Enclosed single mount with ammunition-handling room below. Originally on destroyers, destroyer escorts and auxiliaries. Now mainly found in auxiliary vessels of the US Navy, these single mounts are also the main surface armament of the *Lepanto* class destroyers and *Legazpi* class frigates of the Spanish Navy.
(b) Open single mount with ammunition-handling room below. Auxiliary vessels.
(c) Open single mount without ammunition hoists or handling room. Converted merchant vessels.

In performance there is essentially no difference between the first two of these and one gun of the enclosed twin mounting. The third arrangement is necessarily less efficient in terms of ammunition handling; but otherwise the gun characteristics are the same.

SINGLE 5-inch 54-CALIBRE MARK 39 MOUNTING (USA)

This mounting is an intermediate stage between the 5-inch 38-calibre mountings and the 5-inch 54-calibre Mk 42 mountings. It can be regarded as a 5-inch 38-calibre single enclosed mounting Mk 30 with the Mk 12 38-calibre gun replaced by a Mk 16 54-calibre gun. This gun fires a heavier shell (about 32 kg instead of about 25 kg) with a slightly higher muzzle velocity and thus a longer range.

It may be noted that in this mounting an amplidyne all-electric power drive is used, whereas in both the 5-inch 38-calibre mountings and the 5-inch 54-calibre Mk 42 mountings the drive is electro-hydraulic. The gun was first introduced in 1944.

Status

Installed as a single enclosed mounting in *Midway* class aircraft carriers and seven ships of the Japanese *Murasame* and *Harukaze* classes.

Above: Twin 5-inch 38-calibre gun mounting Mk 32.

Single 5-inch 38-calibre gun mounting on US *Knox* class frigate.

SINGLE 5-inch 54-CALIBRE MARK 42 MOUNTING (USA)

This widely-adopted mounting had several advantages over both the 5-inch 38-calibre mountings and the 5-inch 54-calibre Mk 39 mounting. It uses the Mk 18 54-calibre gun, and it is capable of very much higher rates of fire. Mod 7, which is the most widely used operationally of the earlier versions, is a dual-purpose single enclosed mounting fitted with automatic ammunition feed mechanisms. Driven by electro-hydraulic power units, it can be operated in local or automatic control.

The gun housing slide and breech mechanism are quite different from those of the semi-automatic 5-inch 54-calibre and 5-inch 38-calibre designs, as also is the ammunition feed system which involves manual operations only in loading the cylindrical, power-driven loading drums. As a result the single gun can achieve a continuous firing rate equal to that achieved only in short bursts by an expert crew on the two guns of the 5-inch 38-calibre Mk 32 mounting. The complete turret weighs about 60 tons.

Gun Data
Calibre: 127 mm (5-inch)
Barrel length: 54 calibres
Elevation: to 85°
Projectile weight: approx 32 kg
Muzzle velocity: approx 810 m/sec
Rate of fire: 45 rounds/min
Maximum range: approx 24 km (13 nm)
Maximum altitude: 13,600 m
Date introduced: 1953

Status
Operational in ships of the US Navy and elsewhere. To be mounted on the new *Andalucia* class frigates of the Spanish Navy.

MODIFIED MOD 7 MOUNTING (USA)

In some installations of the Mk 42 the starboard "bubble" or "frog-eye" on the mount has been removed. This dome is normally used for local anti-aircraft control; the port dome, which is retained in these installations, is for local anti-surface control.

Above: 5-inch 54-calibre Mk 42 mounting.

Left: Single 5-inch 54-calibre Mk 42 Mod 7.

Functionally similar to the Mod 7 mount described above, the Mod 9 is an improved design featuring lower mount weight (58,700 kg), nearly 10 per cent lower power consumption and a smaller crew requirement. Improvements incorporated include replacement of electronic components of the earlier mount by solid-state devices. Only two men are needed on the mount as against four for the Mod 7, and the total crew requirement is 12 men instead of 14. The only respect in which the Mod 7 performance is known to be superior is that of elevation acceleration (60°/sec/sec against 40°/sec/sec).

Status

51 units of the above-decks portion of the mount were manufactured by FMC/NOD and supplied for use on DE-1052 class ships. The below-decks portion was produced by the US Navy Naval Ordnance Station, Louisville.

This new gun mounting was designed primarily for installation in new ships, was required to embody all relevant improvements developed over some 30 years since the 5-inch/38 was first introduced and was required to be light, easily maintained and exceptionally reliable. The result requires only one-third of the crew of a 5-inch/38 and with it a single man in a control centre can fire a drum load of 20 shells without help.

Developed by FMC/NOD the mount offers a crew reduction from 14 to six with none on the mount and a weight reduction from 60 to 25 tons. To achieve these reductions, however, the upper elevation limit has been reduced to 65°, the rate of fire to 20 rounds/min and the number of ready service rounds from 40 to 20. Gun characteristics otherwise are believed to be the same as described for the Mk 42 mounting.

Manufacturer

The Northern Ordnance Division of FMC produced the first batch of 33 mounts and was later given an order for ten mounts for Iranian warships. General Electric's Ordnance Systems division has also produced 56 mountings.

Status

In service with the US Navy. Selected as armament for the DD-947, DD-993 and DD-997 classes, plus the CG-47 (formerly DDG-47).

Single 5-inch lightweight Mk 45 mounting.

SINGLE 5-inch MOUNTING

(US/ARGENTINA/CHILE)

A 5-inch (127 mm) gun is mounted on the ex-USS *Brooklyn* class cruisers of the Argentine Navy — and on similar vessels in the Chilean Navy. The gun is a short 25-calibre weapon and is mounted as eight single installations.

These weapons are assumed to be of American manufacture, but 5-inch guns of this type are no longer in service in the US Navy.

Status
Operational but no longer made.

76 mm 62-CALIBRE GUN MOUNT MARK 75

(USA)

The OTO Melara 76 mm gun is now in full production in the USA at the Northern Ordnance Division of FMC. The weapon will be installed on FFG-7 frigates, PHM hydrofoils, Coast Guard cutters and patrol craft being built for the Royal Saudi Navy. A description of the Italian weapon, which is identical with the licence-built US equipment may be found on page 68.

3-inch 50-CALIBRE MOUNTINGS MARKS 27, 33 and 34

(USA)

These 3-inch (76 mm) 50-calibre gun mounts are primarily intended for air defence but can be used also against surface targets. Planned during the Second World War but not completed in time for combat use in that conflict, the mounts have since proved themselves so effective that they have virtually displaced their predecessors — 40 mm twin and quadruple mounts — on combat vessels.

Mks 27 and 33 are twin mounts and Mk 34 a single. Mks 27 and 33 are identical in almost all respects, the main difference being in the slide. All marks use the same gun and similar backing mechanisms, except that in the twin mounts the assemblies are of opposite hand. Some models of the Mk 33 are enclosed twin mounts with an aluminium or glass-fibre reinforced plastic shield, and others again are twins with modifications for installation of a fire-control radar antenna. The Mk 34 mount is an open single with a right-hand slide and loader assembly. Some models of the Mk 34 also are FRP shielded. Mount weights are in the region of 14.5 tons for the twins and 7.5 tons for the Mk 34.

Obsolescent Types
In a few vessels completed at or soon after the 1939-45 war a 70-calibre gun was installed in twin mounts, but it is believed that there are now none in service anywhere.

A much earlier (circa 1936) 3-inch weapon is still to be found in a variety of US auxiliary vessels. Performance is similar to the later weapons except that the achievable rate of fire is much lower.

Gun Data
Calibre: 76 mm (3-inch)
Barrel length: 50 calibres (see above)
Elevation: to 85°
Projectile weight: approx 6 kg
Muzzle velocity: approx 825 m/sec
Rate of fire: 50 rounds/barrel/min
Maximum range: approx 13 km (7 nm)
Maximum altitude: approx 9,000 m

Status
Operational in many ships of the US and other navies.

3-inch 50-calibre mounting Mk 34.

There are single, twin and quadruple barrelled versions of the 40 mm automatic recoil operated gun in service in the US Navy. The gun has a range of approx 5,000 m and a rate of fire of 160 rounds/min. Most mounts can be either locally or remotely controlled, and are power operated, with emergency hand operation. The gun is derived from the Bofors design.

Status
Operational as noted.

(USA)   EMERLEC-30 TWIN 30 mm MOUNTING

Designed for anti-ship, anti-aircraft and anti-missile fire, the Emerlec-30 is a lightweight mounting carrying two 30 mm Oerlikon cannon, an environmentally-controlled cabin for the operator, a day or night sighting system and a supply of below-deck ready-use ammunition. It can be operated under local or remote control and has sufficient on-mount battery power to operate the guns through the firing of a full load of ammunition should the ship's power be interrupted for any reason.

Gun Data
Calibre: 30 mm
Elevation: –15 to +80°
Projectile weight: 0.35 kg
Rate of fire: 600 rounds/barrel/min
Maximum range: 8 km (4 nm)
Mounting weight: 1.9 tons

Manufacturer
Emerson Electric

Status
In service or on order for Ecuador, Greece, Nigeria, South Korea and the Philippines.

40 mm mountings on board a Swiftship 105-foot US Navy fast-patrol craft.

Emerlec-30 twin 30 mm mounting.

20 mm M 197 DECK MOUNT

This system comprises an M 197 three-barrel 20 mm gun and ancillary equipment mounted on a US Navy Mk 10 stand. The gun and its associated delinking feeder (M-89) are used by the USMC in helicopters and in US naval aircraft.

The M 197 weapon is electrically operated and power is supplied by a battery mounted on the gun stand.

The three-barrel gun is derived from the six-barrel M-61 (Vulcan) gun and has alternative rates of fire of 600 and 1,200 rounds/min.

Gun Data
Calibre: 20 mm
Elevation: –15 to +75°
Traverse: unlimited
Ammunition: M-50 Series
Muzzle velocity: 1,030 m/sec
Rate of fire: 600 or 1,200 rounds/min
Ready rounds: 300
Weight on Mk 10 mounting: approx 500 kg

Manufacturer
General Electric

NAVAL VULCAN AIR-DEFENCE SYSTEM

Two naval variants of the well-known six-barrel M-168 gun have been devised by General Electric. Both are primarily intended for close-in defence against air and surface threats but must not be confused with the much more elaborate Vulcan/Phalanx system. Both the EX-80 Mod 0 and the EX-80 Mod 1 have been tested by the US Navy. The former is a self-contained equipment with its own built-in stabilisation system, while the latter can operate either on its own or by taking target-designations from the ship's fire-control system.

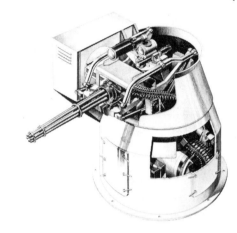

Naval Vulcan air-defence system.

VULCAN/PHALANX

Despite the deployment of a multi-layer defence system consisting of intercepters plus long- and medium-range surface-to-air missiles to protect its warships, the US Navy still feels the need to have a "last-ditch" system capable of engaging incoming vessels or low-level aircraft which have "leaked through" these defences. The resulting Mk 15 Close-In Weapon System (CIWS) is based on the Vulcan land-based anti-aircraft system and relies on a fast reaction time and the ability to saturate the incoming threat with a barrage of accurate cannon fire.

Heart of the system is the well-known 20 mm Gatling-type cannon which for years has formed the gun armament of US fighter aircraft. This proven gun has been mated with a self-contained fire-control system which incorporates closed-loop spotting. The latter feature involves tracking both the incoming target and the outgoing rounds, correcting the aim as necessary to bring the two together. To ensure a high projectile velocity and adequate lethality, the weapon fires discarding-sabot projectiles whose core is made of depleted uranium (known as Staballoy). Maximum rate of fire is 3,000 rounds/min and the mount is free to move through 360° in azimuth and between +90 and -35° in elevation.

Manufacturer
System contractor: General Dynamics Pomona
Status
Operational aboard US Navy warships.

Phalanx defence system shows Vulcan gun with radome for the tracking radar above.

(USA)

General Electric has devised this low-profile mounting to provide firepower for light craft. Developed using many major components from the UTS turret used on the AH-1 Cobra helicopter, the remote-controlled mounting can carry the 7.62 mm M134 machine gun, 20 mm M197 cannon, 30 mm XM188E1 cannon, the 40 mm M19 grenade launcher or a pod containing four General Dynamics Stinger surface-to-air missiles. The remote sighting station can accept a right sight, reflex sight, night-vision sight or a dual-mode gunsight.

(USSR)

These guns are in service with several of the older cruisers of the Russian fleet. The *Sverdlov* class cruisers each carry 12 guns in four triple mountings, except for the *Dzerzhinski* which has had one of its turrets replaced by a launcher for the SAM-2 Guideline missile. The older *Tchapaev* class cruisers also carry four triple turrets.

Guns in the turrets are mounted in separate sleeves, thus permitting individual elevation to at least 50°. An 8 m range-finder is incorporated in each turret and the guns are semi-automatic.

EX-84 UNIVERSAL MOUNT

Gun Data (20 mm version)
Calibre: 20 mm
Elevation: −10 to +55°
Mounting weight: 0.6 tons (including 750 rounds of ammunition)

Manufacturer
General Electric

TRIPLE 152 mm MOUNTING

Gun Data
Calibre: 152 mm
Barrel length: 50 calibres
Elevation: to 50°
Projectile weight: 50 kg
Muzzle velocity: 915 m/sec
Rate of fire: 10 rounds/min
Maximum range: approx 27.5 km (15 nm)
Date introduced: 1938

Status
Operational as noted.

Triple 152 mm mounting on *Sverdlov* class Soviet cruiser.

TWIN 130 mm MOUNTING

These mountings are to be found on the older destroyers of Russian and client navies, notably the *Skory, Tallin* and *Kotlin* classes. The mountings are semi-automatic and said to be fully stabilised. There appear to be some external differences between the mountings on the *Skory* and those on later vessels and it is possible that there may be an earlier, unstabilised mounting on some.

Gun Data
Calibre: 130 mm
Barrel length: 50 calibres
Projectile weight: 27 kg
Muzzle velocity: 875 m/sec
Rate of fire: 10 rounds/min
Maximum range: 25 km (13.5 nm)
Date introduced: 1936

Status
Operational, as noted above.

TWIN 100 mm MOUNTING

Dual-purpose guns of this type are in service with the Russian Navy on the *Sverdlov* class cruisers (including the *Dzerzhinski*) and the *Tchapaev* class cruisers, on which they are associated with Wackel-topf stabilised directors with radar. The turret is stabilised and has been said to weigh 35 tons.

Gun Data
Calibre: 100 mm
Barrel length: 60 calibres
Elevation: to 80°
Projectile weight: 16 kg
Muzzle velocity: 900 m/sec
Rate of fire: 20 rounds/min
Maximum range: 18 km (10 nm)
Maximum altitude: 12,000 m
Date introduced: 1942

Status
Operational as noted.

Twin 130 mm mounting on *Skory* class destroyer.

(USSR)

This mounting is to be found on the two *Kirov* class cruisers, on the many *Riga* and *Kola* class destroyers that are to be found in the navies of both Russia and its client countries, and on the *Don* class support ships.

Although the guns are believed to be of more recent design than those in the twin mountings on the *Sverdlov* and *Tchapaev* cruisers they are manually operated and inferior in performance.

SINGLE 100 mm MOUNTING

Gun Data
Calibre: 100 mm
Barrel length: 50 calibres
Elevation: to 80°
Projectile weight: 13.5 kg
Muzzle velocity: 850 m/sec
Rate of fire: 15 rounds/min
Maximum range: 16 km (8.5 nm)
Maximum altitude: 6,000 m
Date introduced: 1947

Status
Operational but obsolescent.

(USSR)

Two elderly dual-purpose mountings, one single and one twin, are still to be found on some *Kronstadt* class coastal patrol vessels and *Skory* class destroyers respectively. The same gun is probably used in both.

85 mm MOUNTINGS

Gun Data
Calibre: approx 85 mm
Barrel length: approx 50 calibres
Elevation: to 75°
Projectile weight: 9.5 kg
Muzzle velocity: approx 800 m/sec
Rate of fire: 15-20 rounds/min
Maximum range: 14 km (7.5 nm)
Maximum altitude: 9,000 m
Date introduced: 1943

Status
Operational but obsolescent.

Single 100 mm mounting seen in stern view of *Kirov*.

TWIN 76 mm MOUNTING

(USSR)

This is a relatively modern dual-purpose mounting which can be found on the *Kynda* class cruisers, the *Kashin* class destroyers and the *Mirka* and *Petya* class frigates of the Soviet Navy. The mountings are stabilised.

Gun Data
Calibre: 76 mm
Barrel length: 60 calibres
Elevation: to approx 85°
Projectile weight: approx 6 kg
Muzzle velocity: approx 900 m/sec
Rate of fire: 60 rounds/min
Maximum range: 15 km (8 nm)
Maximum altitude: 14,000 m
Date introduced: probably late 1950s

Status
In widespread operational use.

Twin 76 mm mountings on *Krivak* class destroyer.

TWIN 57 mm AUTOMATIC MOUNTING

(USSR)

Several of the most modern Russian warships are equipped with fully-enclosed, fully-automatic 57 mm AA guns in twin mountings. They are found in the *Moskva*, *Kresta*, *Grisha*, *Nanuchka*, *Poti*, *Ugra* and *Chilikin* classes and are radar controlled.

Gun Data
Calibre: 57 mm
Barrel length: 80 calibres
Elevation: to approx 85°
Projectile weight: 2.7 kg
Muzzle velocity: approx 1,000 m/sec
Rate of fire: 120 rounds/barrel/min
Maximum range: 12 km (6.5 nm)
Maximum altitude: 5,000 m
Date introduced: 1960s

Status
Current operational weapon, probably still in production.

Quadruple 57 mm AA mountings are installed in the *Kanin* and *Krupny* classes of Russian destroyer and the *Lama* class supply ships. It is believed that the guns, which in these mountings are arranged as two pairs mounted vertically one above the other, are of similar pattern to those in the twin open mountings seen in many modern or modernised Russian naval vessels. It does, however, appear that the guns in the twin mountings are usually fitted with muzzle brakes. A single mounting, probably of a similar gun (but without muzzle brake) is installed in the modified *Skory* class destroyers and *Sasha* class coastal minesweepers.

Gun Data
Calibre: 57 mm
Barrel length: 70 calibres
Elevation: probably to 85°
Projectile weight: 2.8 kg
Muzzle velocity: approx 950 m/sec
Rate of fire: 120 rounds/min
Maximum range: approx 9 km (5 nm)
Maximum altitude: approx 6,000 m
Date introduced: early 1960s

Status
In widespread operational use.

(USSR)   **QUADRUPLE 45 mm MOUNTING**

These Russian mountings are very similar in appearance to the quadruple 57 mm AA gun mounts described above. They are fitted to some of the older destroyers of the fleet — the *Kildin*, *Kotlin* (unmodified) and *Tallin* classes. They are semi-automatic in operation.

Gun Data
Calibre: 45 mm
Barrel length: 85 calibres
Projectile weight: approx 1.5 kg
Muzzle velocity: approx 1,000 m/sec
Rate of fire: approx 160 rounds/min
Maximum range: 9 km (5 nm)
Maximum altitude: approx 7,000 m
Date introduced: early 1950s

Status
Still operational but obsolescent.

Quadruple twin and single 57 mm mountings on *Krupny* class destroyer.

37 mm MOUNTINGS

Twin 63-calibre AA mountings of various types are found on many of the older cruisers, destroyers and auxiliaries of the Russian Navy. The 37 mm AA calibre was first introduced for naval use, adapted from the army weapon in 1943, but the twin mountings for which data are given here are considerably more modern and are semi-automatic in operation.

SINGLE MOUNTINGS

Single mountings incorporating the earlier version of this weapon are installed in open mountings in the earlier *Skory* class destroyers and *Kronstadt* class submarine chasers, and in enclosed mountings on the T-301 coastal minesweepers.

Gun Data
Calibre: 37 mm
Barrel length: 63 calibres
Projectile weight: 0.7 kg
Muzzle velocity: 880 m/sec
Rate of fire: 150 rounds/min
Maximum range: approx 8 km (4 nm)
Maximum altitude: approx 5,000 m

Status
Operational in many Russian naval vessels. Probably no longer in production.

TWIN 30 mm MOUNTING

A fully-automatic, remote-controlled twin 30 mm AA mounting is installed in missile boats and other small craft in the Russian Navy and in the navies of the many countries to which such vessels have been supplied.

Gun Data
Calibre: 30 mm
Barrel length: 65 calibres
Elevation: to 85°
Muzzle velocity: approx 1,000 m/sec
Rate of fire: approx 500 rounds/min
Maximum range: 3-4,000 m
Date introduced: 1960

Status
In widespread operational use.

Twin 30 mm mounting on *Shershen* fast-attack craft.

(USSR)

Like its US counterpart, the Soviet Navy sees the need for a short-range fast reaction gun capable of taking on incoming missiles or low-flying aircraft which have eluded the longer-range defences. The chosen solution is similar — a small-calibre Gatling-type weapon. This operates in conjunction with the Drum Tilt Radar but no other details of its performance are available. For a long time this weapon was thought to be of 23 mm calibre, but 30 mm now seems more likely.

(USSR)

At least three versions of this light anti-aircraft gun are known to exist. All have two barrels mounted one above the other in a mounting which can be open, semi-enclosed or enclosed. Soviet designation for the first of these is 2-M-3 110PM, and this variant is known to have powered training and elevation but only simple visual sights. The more sophisticated mountings may have some measure of remote control.

CLOSE-IN WEAPON SYSTEM

Status
Operational aboard a wide range of Soviet Navy ships including *Kirov* class battlecruisers, *Kuriles* class aircraft carriers, *Kara* and *Kresta II* class cruisers.

TWIN 25 mm GUN MOUNTING

Gun Data
Calibre: 25 mm
Barrel length: 80 calibres
Elevation: –10 to +85°
Muzzle velocity: 900 m/sec
Rate of fire: probably 270-300 rounds/barrel/min
Mounting weight: 1.5 tons
Date introduced: probably early 1950s

Status
Operational on the smaller patterns of Soviet warship. Some variants may be obsolescent.

Twin 25 mm gun mounting on Soviet torpedo boats.

30 mm Gatling type weapons mounted in pairs guard the stern of the battle cruiser *Kirov*.

BOMBARDMENT ROCKETS

Although the bombardment rocket has a long history as a naval weapon, and despite the growing popularity of multiple rocket launchers among land forces in recent years, there is little apparent enthusiam for such weapons in the world's navies at present. Even the Russians, who have led the field in this department of warfare for more than three decades, have done little to develop their many launchers as naval bombardment weapons.

For anti-submarine purposes, of course, there have been numerous rocket weapon developments, and these are described in the section on ASW weapons. Illuminating flare rockets and, more recently, ECM chaff-dispensing rockets are also to be found, but these are scarcely to be described as weapons.

RAP 14 BOMBARDMENT ROCKET SYSTEM

(FRANCE)

The multiple unguided rocket system known as RAP 14 has been proposed for naval applications. As can be seen from the accompanying picture of a model of the system, the naval version will have a 2 × 9 rocket launcher on a remotely-controlled mounting with provision for automatic reloading from below deck with the launcher in the vertical position. Each of the two magazine drums will contain 36 rockets, giving a total capacity, with a full launcher and full magazine, of 90 rockets. The model shown here is of an installation suitable for ships of the *La Combattante II* type; other configurations are possible.

Weapon Data
Calibre: 140 mm
Launch weight: 54 kg
Warhead: 19 kg HE standard
Speed: Mach 2 maximum
Rate of fire: 9 secs for 18-round salvo; single rounds or smaller salvoes may be fired
Range: 16 km (8.5 nm) standard maximum
CEP: 90 m

Manufacturer
Systems CNIM and in cooperation with Creusot-Loire for the mounting.

Status
Land version fully developed. Naval version proposed.

140 mm ROCKET LAUNCHER

(USSR)

For the past 30 years and more the Russian Army has been using and arranging for the development of a wide range of unguided barrage rockets. It is not surprising, therefore, that the Russian Navy should also use these weapons: indeed it is surprising that they have not made greater use of them.

So far as is known at present the only confirmed installation is on the *Polnocny* class landing ship. This carries a trainable launcher with a capacity for 18 rounds of 140 mm rockets. These are credited with a range of some 9 km (5 nm).

Twin 140 mm rocket launchers aboard *Polnocny* class landing ship.

TORPEDOES

(FRANCE)

Submarine-launched anti-ship (or anti-submarine) torpedo.

TYPE E14

Data
Target: 0-20 kt ship or submarine near surface
Guidance: passive acoustic, 500 m range, with autopilot approach
Length: 429 cm
Diameter: 55 cm
Weight: 900 kg
Propulsion: electric
Speed: 25 kt
Range: 5,500 m (3 nm)
Submersion: pre-set at 6-18 m
Warhead: 200 kg HE
Fuze: contact and electromagnetic

Manufacturer
Cit-Alcatel for DTCN

Status
Quantity production: French Navy service.

(FRANCE)

Submarine-launched anti-ship (or anti-submarine) torpedo.

TYPE E15

Data
Target: 0-20 kt ship or submarine near surface
Guidance: passive acoustic, medium range, with autopilot approach
Length: 600 cm
Diameter: 55 cm
Weight: 1,350 kg
Propulsion: electric
Speed: 25 kt
Range: 12,000 m (6.5 nm)
Submersion: pre-set 6-18 m
Warhead: 300 kg HE
Fuze: contact and electromagnetic

Manufacturer
CIT-Alcatel for DTCN

Status
Quantity production: French Navy service

(FRANCE)

Intended for submarine attacks against surface ships, the new F17 can be launched in wire-guided or automatic mode. Final attack phase is normally carried out in homing mode and the parent submarine can switch the torpedo from one mode to another. The multi-mode F17P has a seeking head capable of operating on active or passive mode.

TYPE F17

Data
Target: surface vessels
Guidance: wire and automatic homing
Length: 591 cm
Diameter: 53.5 cm
Weight: 1,410 kg
Propulsion: electric

Manufacturer
DTCN

Status
In the early stages of production.

TYPE L3 (FRANCE)

Ship-launched or submarine-launched anti-submarine torpedo.

Data
Target: submarine up to 20 kt and down to 300 m
Guidance: acoustic, active, 600 m range in good conditions. Pre-programmed circular or helical (deep water) search pattern if target not detected after predicted time
Length: 430 cm
Diameter: 55 cm
Weight: 910 kg
Propulsion: electric
Speed: 25 kt
Range: 5,500 m (3 nm)
Submersion: 300 m maximum
Warhead: 200 kg HE
Fuze: contact and acoustic proximity

Manufacturer
DTCN

Status
In service with the French Navy.

TYPE L4 (FRANCE)

Anti-submarine torpedo designed to be launched from aircraft or the Malafon ASW missile. Special devices to ensure smooth entry into the water. A modernised version capable of operating in shallow water is now available.

Data
Target: submerged submarines up to 20 kt
Guidance: active acoustic homing preceded by circular search
Length: 313 cm including parachute-stabiliser
Diameter: 55.3 cm
Weight: 540 kg
Propulsion: electric
Speed: 30 kt
Fuze: impact and acoustic proximity

Manufacturer
DTCN

Status
In service with the French Navy.

TYPE L5 MULTI-PURPOSE TORPEDO (FRANCE)

Several models of the Type L5 have now been developed.

Mod 1   for use on surface vessels
Mod 3   for submarine use
Mod 4   anti-submarine torpedo
Mod 4P multi-purpose torpedo

All are fitted with a Thomson-CSF active/passive seeker head which can direct the weapon into direct attacks or programme searches using either active or passive homing.

Data
Target: surface vessels or submarines (see above)
Guidance: active/passive acoustic homing
Diameter: 53.3 cm
Weight: Mod 1   1,000 kg
          Mod 3   1,300 kg
          Mod 4   1,000 kg
          Mod 4P 1,000 kg
Propulsion: electric

Manufacturer
DTCN

Status
All versions are operational, the Mod 4 and 4P being in French and foreign service.

TYPE Z16

This free-running submarine-launched torpedo travels a pre-set course, switching to a zig-zag pattern if no target is encountered by the time it reaches a pre-determined distance.

Data
Target: surface vessels
Guidance: pre-set
Length: 720 cm
Diameter: 55 cm
Weight: 1,700 kg
Propulsion: electric
Speed: 30 kt
Range: 10 km (5.4 nm)
Submersion: down to 18 m
Warhead: 300 kg
Fuze: contact or magnetic proximity

Status
Obsolescent.

(WEST GERMANY)

SEEAL/SST 4

The SEEAL ship- or submarine-launched weapon was developed in parallel with the Seeschlange in the 1960s to meet the requirements of the West German Navy. The export-model SST 4 (Special Surface Target) is comparable in dimensions and performance.

SEEAL/SST 4 on test rig.

Data
Target: surface vessels
Guidance: active/passive acoustic homing plus wire
Length: 640 cm (including wire-dispenser casket)
Diameter: 53.3 cm
Weight: 1,370 kg
Propulsion: electric
Warhead: 260 kg
Fuze: contact or magnetic proximity

Manufacturer
AEG Telefunken

Status
SEEAL is operational aboard West German Navy Class 206 submarines and Type 142 and 143 fast-attack craft. SST 4 is in service with eight navies in NATO and South America aboard Class 209 submarines and *Jaguar* and *Combattante II* and *III* fast-attack craft.

SEESCHLANGE

(WEST GERMANY)

Seeschlange differs from the Seal in being intended for anti-submarine use. It has half the battery capacity of Seal but is fitted with a three-dimensional sonar seeker.

Data
Target: submarines
Guidance: three-dimensional active/passive acoustic seeker plus wire
Length: 400 cm (including wire-dispenser casket)
Diameter: 53.3 cm
Propulsion: electric
Warhead: 100 kg
Fuze: contact or magnetic proximity

Manufacturer
AEG Telefunken

Status
Operational with the West German Navy aboard Class 206 submarines.

SURFACE AND UNDERWATER TARGET (SUT)

(WEST GERMANY)

A further development of Seal, SUT is a dual-purpose weapon capable of tackling surface targets or those operating at the maximum depth capability of conventional submarines. The use of inertial guidance allows self-guidance attacks to be carried out once the target has been acquired. Wire guidance permits the two-way exchange of data between launch platform and torpedo, and even the final attack portion of the trajectory can be controlled by the parent vessel.

Data
Target: surface vessels or submarines
Guidance: wire, inertial and active/passive acoustic homing
Length: 613 cm (670 cm including the wire-dispensing casket)
Diameter: 53.3 cm

Manufacturer
AEG Telefunken

Status
In production.

TYPE A.184

(ITALY)

Suitable for surface-vessel or submarine launching, the A.184 light-weight torpedo combines wire guidance with an advanced pattern of active/passive homing head. Powered by a dual-speed electric motor, it can operate at considerable depths.

Data
Target: surface vessels or submarines
Guidance: wire plus active/passive acoustic homing
Length: 600 cm
Diameter: 53.3 cm
Weight: 1,300 kg
Propulsion: electric
Warhead: HE

Manufacturer
Whitehead Moto Fides

Status
In production.

(ITALY)

TYPE A.244

Intended for use in normal or shallow water, the A.244 uses an active/passive homing head whose design contains features intended to offer good resistance to acoustic reverberation. The improved A.244/S has a head of even more advanced design for increased anti-reverberation and anti-countermeasures performance.

Data
Target: submarines
Guidance: active/passive acoustic homing
Length: 270 cm
Diameter: 32.4 cm
Weight: 000 kg
Propulsion: electric

Manufacturer
Whitehead Moto Fides

Status
In production.

(ITALY)

TYPE G6e

Ship-launched or submarine-launched anti-ship torpedo.

Data
Target: surface vessels
Guidance: wire with passive acoustic homing
Length: 600 cm
Diameter: 53.3 cm
Propulsion: electric
Warhead: 300 kg HE
Fuze: contact

Manufacturer
Whitehead Moto Fides

Status
Certainly obsolescent and probably obsolete.

Type A.184 lightweight torpedo.

TYPE G62ef

Submarine-launched anti-submarine device comprising the main body of the (obsolete) Whitehead G6e wire-guided torpedo with an American Mk 44 lightweight (324 mm) torpedo in place of the G6e warhead and homing device. The combination is known as the G62ef or Kangaroo torpedo.

Data
Target: submerged submarines
Guidance: wire run-out of G6e followed by Mk 44 ejection and search-and-homing by active sonar
Length: 620 cm including the Mk 44 payload
Propulsion: electric

Manufacturer
System: Whitehead Moto Fides

Status
Certainly obsolescent and probably obsolete.

TYPE 41

Ship-launched or submarine-launched lightweight dual-purpose torpedo with special ability to operate in shallow water or in otherwise acoustically difficult conditions. Simple to operate and easily installed in almost any vessel from a fishing boat upwards.

Data
Target: ships or submarines
Guidance: active homing sonar giving both azimuth and depth guidance
Length: 244 cm
Diameter: 40 cm
Weight: 250 kg
Propulsion: electric
Fuze: impact and proximity

Manufacturer
Forenade Fabriksverken

Status
In service with the Royal Swedish Navy.

TYPE 42

Lightweight all-purpose torpedo generally similar in concept to the Type 41 but with the additional facility of launching without a parachute from helicopters and with the option of add-on wire guidance.

Data
Target: ships or submarines
Guidance: active homing sonar giving both azimuth and depth guidance. Optional added wire guidance
Length: 244 cm (plus 18 cm for optional wire section)
Diameter: 40 cm
Weight: 300 kg
Propulsion: electric
Fuze: impact and proximity

Manufacturer
Forenade Fabriksverken

Status
In production (after extensive proving trials) for the Royal Swedish Navy.

Type 42 lightweight all-purpose torpedo.

(SWEDEN)

TYPE 61

Ship-launched or submarine-launched long-range anti-ship torpedo.

Type 61 long-range torpedo.

Data
Target: surface vessels
Guidance: wire
Length: 702.5 cm
Diameter: 53.3 cm
Launch weight: 1,765 kg
Propulsion: thermal, low wake, using hydrogen
peroxide as oxidizer
Warhead: 250 kg HE
Fuze: impact and proximity

Manufacturer
Forenade Fabriksverken

Status
Produced in large numbers for the Royal Swedish Navy and for some NATO navies. Operational.

(UK)

MARK 8

Ship-launched or submarine-launched free-running anti-ship torpedo. Originally developed in the early 1930s.

Recovering a Mk 8 torpedo.

Data
Target: surface vessels
Guidance: free-running with mechanically pre-set
depth and course angles
Length: 670 cm
Diameter: 53.3 cm
Weight: 1,535 kg
Propulsion: compressed air
Speed: 45 kt
Range: 4.5 km (2 nm)
Submersion: to 18 m

Status
Obsolescent. Being replaced in Royal Navy service by Tigerfish torpedo.

MARK 20 IMPROVED   (UK)

Originally intended to be a weapon for use against both surface ships and submarines, the Mk 20 as it now exists is an anti-submarine torpedo, the performance of the homing head against surface targets never having been successful. The planned Mk 22 development incorporating umbilical-cable setting of attack data instead of the existing spindle-setting system was cancelled by the British Government but the manufacturer went on to produce the new variant for export.

Data
Target: submarines
Guidance: passive acoustic homing
Length: 411 cm
Diameter: 53.3 cm
Weight: 820 kg
Propulsion: electric (perchloric acid battery)
Speed: 20 kt
Range: 11 km (6 nm) at 20 kt
Submersion: maximum homing depth 244 m
Warhead: 91 kg HE
Fuze: contact

Manufacturer
Vickers Shipbuilding Group

Status
Obsolescent.

MARK 23   (UK)

Developed as an interim weapon and eventual training round, the Mk 23 was the Royal Navy's first wire-guided torpedo. It consists basically of a Mk 20 extended in length to house a wire-guidance dispensing system. Final guidance is by means of a passive acoustic homing head and the range is reported to be around 8 km.

Manufacturer
Vickers Shipbuilding Group

Status
Remains in service with the Royal Navy and other operators.

MARK 24 TIGERFISH   (UK)

The story of post-war British torpedo development has not been a happy one, repeated delays resulting in a series of weapons entering service when already obsolescent. The Mk 24 was originally conceived to meet a 1959 requirement and was expected to enter service in the mid-1960s. First production rounds did not see service until 1974 due to a protracted development programme, so the weapon's ability to cope with the likely threats of the 1980s seems questionable.

Now known as Tigerfish, the Mk 24 is a roll-stabilised weapon which combines the use of wire guidance with a three-dimensional homing head. Wire is paid out from both the torpedo and the parent vessel so as to reduce the stress caused by their relative motion. Two models are known to exist — the original Mod 0 and the later Mod 1 which entered service in 1978.

Data
Target: surface vessels and submarines
Guidance: wire plus active/passive acoustic homing
Length: 646 cm
Diameter: 53.3 cm
Weight: 1,550 kg
Propulsion: electric, two speed via contra-rotating propellors
Range: minimum 32 km (17.4 nm) (estimated)
Fuze: impact and proximity

Manufacturer
Marconi Space and Defence Systems

Status
In production for the Royal Navy.

NAVAL STAFF TARGET 7525   (UK)

Feasibility studies for a new heavy torpedo to replace the Tigerfish (Mk 24) were completed in 1980. Marconi Space and Defence Systems hopes to apply experience gained during the development of the Stingray lightweight torpedo to a new weapon capable of meeting the requirements of Naval Staff Target 7525, but the US-based Gould Corporation claims that the latest version of its Mk 48 can meet the requirement on a shorter timescale and at a lower cost. Selection of the Marconi weapon was announced in September 1981.

Under development by Marconi Space and Defence Systems as a replacement for US Mk 44 and Mk 46 torpedoes in Royal Navy service, Stingray is fitted with an on-board digital computer which enables the autonomous acquisition, classification and tracking of targets. The computer selects the optimum combination of sonar modes to suit the prevailing acoustic conditions including the presence of any countermeasures. Propulsion is by means of a quiet electric motor coupled to a sea-water-electrolyte battery, and the weapon may be used in very shallow water or against deep-diving targets.

Stingray lightweight torpedo being released from Royal Navy Sea King helicopter.

Stingray.

Tigerfish Mk 24.

ADVANCED ASW TORPEDO

Originally known as the Advanced Lightweight Torpedo, this weapon is intended to meet the threat posed by the deeper-diving faster and quieter submarines of the 1980s and beyond. It will be suitable for launching from surface vessels, submarines and aircraft.

CAPTOR

(USA)

Captor is an anti-submarine weapon consisting of a modified Mk 46 torpedo mounted in a mine casing. Developed by Goodyear Aerospace, it is intended for sowing in deep water in the vicinity of routes travelled by hostile submarines, and is capable of discriminating between submarine targets and surface vessels. Heart of this discrimination system is the Detection and Control Unit (DCU) which detects possible targets, identifies them by sound signature and launches the torpedo once a suitable target is within range. (Maximum acquisition range of the Mk 46 homing head is estimated as 460 m.) Deployed life of the weapon is around six months, but it does not remain active for the entire period. The DCU also has the task of turning the weapon off and on as required.

The programme dates back to the late 1960s and operational evaluation was completed in 1975. Follow-on tests were carried out in the late 1970s with the aim of ensuring long-term reliability, but the production rate was kept to a minimum and temporarily suspended when the level of effectiveness remained below expectation. Research and development is continuing in the hope of improving the weapon, but parallel studies are being carried out to examine alternative methods of providing a deep-water mine system.

DEXTOR

(USA)

Little has been released concerning this project to develop a torpedo capable of dealing with deep-diving nuclear submarines. Test launches of experimental hardware were carried out from the submarine USS *Dolphin* in 1969 but no further trials have been reported since.

The project should not be confused with Extor (now known as Submarine Weapons Stowage/Launch), a project to increase the weapon-carrying capacity of SSN-688 class nuclear submarines by mounting additional weaponry outside the pressure hull.

FREEDOM TORPEDO

(USA)

This private-venture Westinghouse weapon can be surface- or submarine-launched for use against surface targets. Two models are available, the Mod 0 with a programmed terminal pattern and the Mod 1 with a long-range homing system. Being 48.3 cm in diameter, it can swim out of 53.3 cm torpedo tubes.

Data
Target: surface vessels
Guidance: wire with terminal pattern (Mod 0) or long-range homing (Mod 1)
Length: 572 cm
Diameter: 48.3 cm
Weight: 1,160 kg
Propulsion: electric from 9-min seawater battery
Speed: 40 kt
Range: 10-14 km (5.4-7.5 nm)
Submersion: 2-15 m
Warhead: minimum 295 kg
Fuze: contact

Manufacturer
Westinghouse Defence and Electronic Systems

Status
Private venture.

(USA)

MARK 14

Submarine-launched anti-ship torpedo which has been in service for some 40 years. Current model is Mk 14 Mod 5.

Data (Mod 5)
Target: surface vessels
Guidance: pre-set depth and course angles
Length: 525 cm
Diameter: 53.3 cm
Weight: 1,780 kg
Propulsion: alcohol-burning thermal engine/compressed air
Speed: 32-46 kt
Range: 4.6-9 km (2.58-5 nm)
Submersion: to 18 m
Warhead: 230 kg

Status
Operational in the USN and elsewhere.

(USA)

MARK 27

This passive-homing torpedo was used primarily as a training round by the US Navy but some were supplied as operational weapons to a number of overseas navies.

Data
Target: surface vessels and submarines
Guidance: passive acoustic homing
Length: 323 cm
Diameter: 48.3 cm
Propulsion: electric

Status
May still be in service with overseas customers, but is no longer used by the US Navy.

(USA)

MARK 32

Although no longer used by the US Navy, this acoustic-homing torpedo is still operational aboard ex-USN escort vessels transferred to other navies. Current version is the active-homing Mk 32 Mod 2.

Data
Target: submarines
Guidance: active acoustic homing
Length: 208 kg
Diameter: 48.3 cm
Weight: 350 kg
Propulsion: electric (silver/zinc oxide battery)
Range: approx 8 km (4 nm) at 12 kt
Warhead: 49 kg HE

Status
Obsolete but still in limited service.

MARK 37   (USA)

Ship-launched or submarine-launched dual-purpose (but see below) torpedo. Can be deck-launched using Mk 23 and Mk 25 torpedo launchers; and for submarine launching the torpedo is fitted with guides which enable it to fit into, and swim out from, a standard 21-inch tube.

Two distinct versions of the torpedo have been built, each of which has two model numbers. Mods 0 and 3 are free-running torpedoes with active and passive sonar homing: Mods 1 and 2 are wire-guided.

Although intended for use against both surface and submerged targets, the Mk 37 has been used primarily in an anti-submarine role because of the difficulties associated with sonar homing against surface targets.

Data (Mods 0 and 3)
Target: mainly submarines
Guidance: pre-set depth and course angle for run-out followed by active, passive or active/passive sonar homing with or without preliminary search pattern
Length: 352 cm
Diameter: 48.3 cm
Weight: 648 kg
Propulsion: electric (silver-zinc battery)
Speed: 30 kt
Range: 7 km (4 nm)
Submersion: maximum homing depth 370 m
Warhead: 150 kg HE
Fuze: impact
Date introduced: 1952

Mods 1 and 2 as Mods 0 and 3 except –
Guidance: wire run-out
Length: 409 cm
Weight: 766 kg
Date introduced: 1961

Status
Remains operational with the US Navy.

MARK 44   (USA)

Ship-launched or air-launched lightweight anti-submarine torpedo. Has been used as the payload of the ASROC missile and the G62ef Kangaroo torpedo combination by the Italian Navy. Deck launching is from Mk 32 tubes.

Data
Target: submarines
Guidance: depth and course settings by umbilical cable; active acoustic homing
Length: 256 cm
Diameter: 32.4 cm
Weight: 233 kg
Propulsion: electric
Speed: approx 30 kt
Range: 5 km (2.5 nm)
Submersion: maximum homing depth 300 m
Warhead: 40 kg HE
Date introduced: 1960

Status
Obsolescent. Replaced by Mk 46 in US and UK and generally being replaced in other countries.

MARK 46   (USA)

This ship-launched or air-launched anti-submarine torpedo was developed as a replacement for the earlier Mk 44. Two versions were originally developed — the Mod 0 using a solid-propellant motor and the Mod 1 with a liquid-monopropellant (Otto) motor. The Mod 1 is lighter than the Mod 0 and was selected for deployment, entering service in 1967. The Mod 2 became operational in 1972.

Current improvement efforts are concentrated on the NEARTIP project, which is aimed at overcoming the effect of sound-absorbing (anechoic) coatings (code-named Clusterguard) applied to some Soviet Navy submarines, and also improves resistance to countermeasures. The Mk 46 is also used as the payload of the Captor mine but requires slight modifications for this role.

Data
Target: submarines
Guidance: active/passive acoustic homing
Length: 259 cm
Diameter: 32.4 cm
Weight: 230 kg
Propulsion: liquid monopropellant
Range: 11 km (6 nm)
Submersion: maximum homing depth 450 m
Warhead: 40 kg HE

Manufacturer
Aerojet Electro Systems. Honeywell and Gould Ocean Systems have also been involved in manufacture.

Status
In service with the US Navy, Royal Navy and other operators.

(USA)   MARK 48

This highly-sophisticated torpedo is the standard armament of US Navy submarines. Originally planned as an anti-submarine weapon, it was developed into a dual-role anti-ship and anti-submarine torpedo. Although not in service aboard surface ships, it could be adapted for this role. Propulsion is by means of a liquid-monopropellant (Otto) motor which gives a maximum speed of 93 km/h. A wide range of guidance modes is available, including wire-guidance, active, passive or active/passive acoustic homing. Hughes Aircraft was awarded a contract in 1979 to develop the Adcap (Advanced Capability) version of the Mk 48. This programme will add a new digital guidance and control system to existing torpedoes, maintaining their effectiveness through the 1990s.

Data
Target: surface vessels and submarines
Guidance: active, passive or active/passive acoustic homing plus wire
Length: 580 cm
Diameter: 53.3 cm
Weight: approx 1,600 kg
Propulsion: liquid monopropellant
Speed: 93 kt
Range: 46 km
Submersion: maximum operating depth greater than 900 m

Manufacturer
Gould Incorporated

Status
In service with the US Navy since 1972. Also procured by the Royal Australian and Royal Netherlands Navies.

Mk 48 torpedo, standard armament of US Navy submarines.

NORTHROP 37C

Ship-launched or submarine-launched dual-purpose torpedo. Derived directly from the standard US Mk 37 (Mods 2 and 3) torpedoes by modification, the 37C is also made in free-running and wire-guided versions.

Major elements of the modification are the replacement of the battery-electric propulsion system by an Otto fuel motor of the type used in the Mk 46/1 torpedo, improvements to the acoustics system to increase sonar detection probability and modification of the logic to give three attack modes — A, straight run anti-ship without homing; B, as A but with delayed search-and-home for lost target; C, full anti-submarine search-and-home.

Performance data have not been published but the following are estimated.

Data
Target: submarines or surface vessels
Guidance: modified Mk 37 (see text)
Dimensions: believed to be substantially the same as Mk 37
Propulsion: liquid monopropellant (Otto) motor
Speed: 42 kt
Range: 14 km (7.5 nm)
Submersion: maximum homing depth 370 m
Warhead: 150 kg HE
Fuze: impact

Manufacturer
Originally developed and manufactured by Northrop, which several years ago sold its interest in the project to Honeywell. The latter company is now responsible for future production.

Status
Operational with the navies of Canada, the Netherlands, Norway and several Middle Eastern and South American nations.

Northrop 37C.

53.3 cm TORPEDO

Standard calibre for Soviet heavy torpedoes is 53.3 cm, launch tubes for weapons of this type being fitted to a wide range of submarines and surface craft. It is likely that a family of weapons exist in this calibre, having been introduced into service at different times — a view encouraged by the fact that some patterns of launch tubes fitted to surface vessels are longer than others. Specialised anti-submarine and anti-ship weapons are thought to exist, including a torpedo with a nuclear warhead which was deployed in the late 1950s. The only torpedo whose designation is known is the Model 1957, with an overall length of 825 cm.

Many classes of Soviet warship carry launch tubes for 40.3 cm diameter torpedoes — weapons thought to be for anti-submarine use. The launch tube is reported to be about 5 m long. Surface vessels carry trainable tubes mounted either singly or in groups of up to five, while submarines such as the *Echo*, *Foxtrot*, *Juliet* and *November* classes carry the weapon in internally-mounted stern tubes. It is not known whether this weapon is also carried by aircraft. Some sources have reported that ASW submarines and helicopters carry weapons of 45 cm diameter — the calibre used by the Soviet Navy during the Second World War. Both calibres would fit within the confines of the torpedo-carrying FRAS-1 and SS-N-14 anti-submarine missiles.

ANTI-SUBMARINE WEAPONS

(AUSTRALIA)   IKARA

A long-range anti-submarine weapon system comprising a guided, powered vehicle and an acoustic homing torpedo. The vehicle is launched from a surface vessel and is powered by a dual-thrust solid-propellant rocket motor. It has short cropped-delta wings, elevon control surfaces and upper and lower vertical tail fins. The payload is a lightweight torpedo (typically the American Mk 44).

Target data, from own ship's sonar or elsewhere, is computed to determine target position; the vehicle is launched from its trainable launcher and radar tracked and radio guided to a torpedo dropping position near the target. The torpedo is dropped by parachute on receipt of a command signed from the launching vessel: on entering the water it executes a search pattern to locate the target and then homes on it.

Initial design was by the Australian Department of Supply and Department of the Navy; and the version installed in Australian ships has its own autonomous digital computer. *RN Ikara* is a version adopted by the Royal Navy in which computer service is provided by the ship's Action Data Automation System. *Branik* is a version developed in the US for the Brazilian *Niteroi* class Mk 10 frigates with a different method of providing computer service.

Missile Data
Length: 343 cm
Wing span: 153 cm
Propulsion: solid-propellant rocket
Guidance: autopilot with altimeter, plus command
Warhead: Mk 44 or Mk 46 homing torpedo
Maximum range: 15-18 km (8-9.7 nm)
Cruising speed: subsonic

Manufacturer
Australian Department of Manufacturing Industry

Status
Operational with the navies of Australia, Brazil and the United Kingdom.

(FRANCE)   MALAFON ANTI-SUBMARINE DRONE SYSTEM

Torpedo-carrying winged drone system primarily designed for use from surface vessels against submarines but suitable for use against surface targets.

The missile is ramp-launched from a trainable launcher and is propelled by two solid-fuel boosters for the first few seconds of flight. Subsequent flight is unpowered but radio-command guided and controlled in altitude by a radio altimeter to maintain a nearly flat trajectory.

At about 800 m from the estimated target position a tail parachute is deployed to decelerate the missile and eject the torpedo payload to complete its mission by acoustic homing.

The drone and launcher are associated with a suitable fire-control system and appropriate target sensors. Flares on the drone wingtips aid tracking for guidance.

Development started in 1956, and although final evaluation and operational trials did not take place until 1964-65 some installations (referred to as Malafon Mk 1) were made before this.

Missile Data
Length: 615 cm
Diameter: 65 cm
Wing span: 330 cm
Launch weight: 1,450 kg
Maximum range: approx 13 km (7 nm)

Manufacturer
Société Industrielle d'Aviation Latécoère

Status
Operational in the French Navy.

Above: Ikara anti-submarine weapon system aboard HMS *Bristol*.

Below: Malafon anti-submarine drone system.

(FRANCE)

A French version of the Swedish Bofors AS rocket system has been developed and produced by Creusot-Loire and is installed in many French warships.

Mechanically, the main innovation is the extension of the system to a six-tube remotely-controlled, automatically-reloaded launcher. With this is associated a CIT-Alcatel sonar and a Thomson-CSF computer to predict future submarine position and calculate the current launcher attitude. The system can use the complete range of Bofors 375 mm AS rockets (brief details of which are listed in the description of the Bofors system) and the computer calculates ballistics for initial velocities of 70, 90, 100 and 130 m/sec as required by the various rockets to give ranges from about 260 m to about 3,600 m.

(NORWAY)

This system uses a rocket-propelled depth charge fired from a remotely-controlled, automatically-loaded six-round launcher. The launcher is controlled by a fire-control system which accepts sonar data for the prediction of the target's future position and computes the rocket ballistics to determine the launcher attitude. The launch rails are pivoted about two axes to give an all-round launch cone. The launcher design provides special protection to enable the weapon to be used in arctic conditions. Fuzing of the projectiles is by proximity, impact and time.

375 mm ANTI-SUBMARINE ROCKET SYSTEM

Launcher Data
Weight: approx 16 tons excluding rockets but including remote control
Traverse: 350°
Elevation: 0-92.5°
Rate of fire: 1 round/sec

Manufacturer
Launcher: Creusot-Loire

Status
In service with the French Navy.

TERNE III ANTI-SUBMARINE ROCKET SYSTEM

Weapon Data
Calibre: 200 mm
Length: 200 cm
Weight: 120 kg
Rate of fire: 6-round salvo in 5 sec
Reload: automatic from magazine, 40 sec
Firing sector: 360°
Range: probably 3,000 m
Date introduced: 1961

Manufacturer
Kongsberg Vaapenfabrikk

Status
Operational in the Royal Norwegian Navy.

Terne III anti-submarine rocket system under test on a US Navy evaluation frigate.

375 mm ANTI-SUBMARINE ROCKET SYSTEM

This system comprises a shipborne rocket launcher having two or more launch tubes, shipborne sonar and a fire-control system. Sonar data on submarine position are used to determine the launcher elevation and bearing angles and the firing system permits the launching of rockets either singly or in salvoes. A special design of missile nose ensures a predictable and accurate under-water trajectory. The launcher is reloaded by automatic means from the magazine which is disposed directly below the launcher.

Missiles have three types of rocket motor giving differing range brackets. The missile trajectory is flat thus giving a short time of flight to minimise target evasive action. Fuses are fitted with hydro-static and DA devices.

The initial version of the system, comprising a four-tube launcher and the M/50 rocket, was developed by AB Bofors in the early 1950s, and became operational about 1956. A two-tube launcher was developed in 1969-73. A version made in France by Creusot-Loire under licence from Bofors has a six-tube launcher and entered service with the French Navy in 1967.

Data
2-tube launcher
Weight: 3.8 tons excluding rockets
Traverse: unlimited
Elevation: 0-60° (firing), 0-90° (loading)
Angular speed: 30°/sec

4-tube launcher
Weight: 7.3 tons excluding rockets
Traverse: ±130°
Elevation: 15-60° (firing), 15-90° (loading)
Angular speed: 18°/sec

Rockets
M/50: 250 kg: range 300-830 m
Erika: 250 kg: range 600-1,600 m
Nelli: 230 kg: range 1,520-3,600 m

Manufacturer
Design and manufacture of basic system by AB Bofors. French version of the system designed and built by Creusot-Loire

Status
In widespread use in the Swedish, French and many other navies.

AB Bofors 375 mm anti-submarine rocket system.

(USA)

This American-designed weapon is no longer in service with the USN but still equips at least the *Akizuki* class destroyers and *Isuzu* class frigates of the Japanese Navy.

It consists of a turret-mounted 324 mm diameter launch tube (Mk 108) from which is projected an anti-submarine rocket weighing 227 kg. The launcher is automatically reloaded, is capable of a high repetition rate and has an almost circular field of fire.

WEAPON ALPHA ANTI-SUBMARINE ROCKET

Weapon Data
Calibre: 324 mm
Rocket weight: 227 kg
Rate of fire: 15 rounds/min
Maximum range: approx 800 m

Status
Obsolescent. Still in service but surpassed by more recent developments. "Weapon Alpha" was formerly known as "Weapon Able", the progression in title reflecting the change in the phonetic spelling of the letter A.

Weapon Alpha anti-submarine rocket launched from a US destroyer.

ASROC ANTI-SUBMARINE ROCKET SYSTEM

This long-range anti-submarine weapon consists of a ship-launched ballistic missile with alternative payloads of an acoustic homing torpedo (Mk 46) or a nuclear depth charge. Associated with the missile and the various launchers that can be used with it are a sonar system and a computer to process the sonar data and missile ballistics to determine the missile launch angles. After the initial boost by its solid-fuel motor the missile sheds the booster and follows a ballistic trajectory to a pre-determined distance from the predicted target position. At this point the payload is separated from the missile body and either parachuted to the surface, if it is a torpedo, or allowed to plunge into the sea if it is a depth charge.

Various launchers can be used, the standard being an eight-cell device and recognised alternatives a combined ASROC/Terrier launcher and the Mk 26 dual-purpose launcher of the Aegis system.

Missile Data
Length: 457 cm
Diameter: 32.5 cm
Fin span: 84.5 cm
Launch weight: 435 kg
Range: believed to be from approx 2 km to 11 km (1-6 nm)
Date introduced: 1961

Manufacturer
Honeywell

Status
Operational in the USN and in the navies of Brazil, Canada, Greece, Indonesia, Iran, Italy, Japan, Spain, Taiwan, Turkey and West Germany.

ASROC anti-submarine rocket system launched from USS *Brinkley*.

SUBROC anti-submarine system after launch from a submerged submarine.

(USA)

SUBROC

SUBROC is a submarine-launched anti-submarine rocket carrying a nuclear depth bomb and forming part of an advanced system designed for deployment in nuclear-powered attack submarines operating against nuclear-powered ballistic missile submarines. Each carries four to six rounds.

Associated with the missile is an elaborate sonar and fire-control system which programmes the missile's inertial navigation system. The missile is launched conventionally and horizontally from the submarine's 21-inch torpedo tubes and at a safe distance from the submarine the solid-fuel missile motor is ignited. After a short continuation of its horizontal motion it is steered upwards and clear of the water.

Throughout its powered flight, both in the water and in the air, the missile is guided by jet deflectors controlled by its inertial navigator. At a pre-determined point, however, the rocket is separated from the bomb and the latter continues on an unpowered trajectory towards the water re-entry point. During this part of the flight the bomb is guided aerodynamically by vanes. Impact with the water is cushioned, to protect the arming and detonation devices, and the bomb is detonated at a pre-determined depth in the vicinity of the target.

Work on a SUBROC improvement programme began in 1976-77 to maintain the weapon's effectiveness against new threats.

Missile Data
Length: 625 cm
Diameter: maximum 533 mm (21-inch)
Launch weight: approx 1,850 kg
Warhead: nuclear depth bomb
Range: 55 km (30 nm)
Date introduced: 1965

Manufacturer
Goodyear Aerospace

Status
Operational in USN nuclear attack submarines.

(USSR)

FRAS-1

This ASROC-type unguided rocket is deployed aboard *Moskva* class helicopter carriers on which it is fired using the forward-mounted SUW-N-1 launcher.

Missile Data
Length: approx 620 cm
Body diameter: 55 cm
Launch weight: approx 1,500 kg
Propulsion: solid-propellant rocket
Guidance: none
Warhead: nuclear depth charge
Maximum range: 25 km

SS-N-14

This winged missile is similar in concept to Malafon and Ikara in that it carries a lightweight anti-submarine torpedo to the approximate location of the submarine target, then drops it into the water. The weapon may also have an anti-ship role, if the torpedo payload has a homing head capable of responding to surface vessels as well as submarines.

Missile Data
Length: 600 cm
Body diameter: 60 cm
Wing span: 150 cm
Propulsion: probably solid-propellant rocket
Guidance: pre-programmed autopilot
Warhead: acoustic homing torpedo
Maximum range: 55 km

Status
In service with the Soviet Navy aboard *Kiev* class aircraft carriers, *Moskva* class helicopter carriers and *Kirov* class battlecruisers (all with a single steerable launcher); *Kara* class cruisers (2 quadruple fixed launchers), *Kresta II* class cruisers (two quadruple fixed launchers) and *Krivak* class destroyers (one quadruple fixed launcher).

SS-N-15

This SUBROC class weapon has a range of 40 km and is deployed aboard *Victor* class submarines. The warhead is thought to be a nuclear depth charge, but no other details are available.

SS-N-16

Very little is known about this submarine-launched anti-submarine weapon beyond the fact that its payload is a homing torpedo. It may be a variant of the SS-N-15.

RUSSIAN ANTI-SUBMARINE ROCKET LAUNCHERS

The Russians do not appear to have adopted the streamlined depth charge of the kind introduced by the Americans in the 1940s. Instead they appear to have leap-frogged a development stage and proceeded directly from the slow-sinking depth-charge to the medium-range anti-submarine rocket.

The development of this type of weapon by the Russians was first noticed by outside observers around 1960. The earliest installation appears to have a small (150 cm long) twin launcher for rockets with a range of 600-800 m. This may still be found on the old *Kola* class frigates, and *Kronstadt* class submarine chasers. More recently a range of more powerful weapons has been introduced: these are described in the entries below.

300 mm ANTI-SUBMARINE ROCKET LAUNCHERS

These long-range Russian anti-submarine rocket launchers have been reported in two slightly different forms. Both are six-barrel, pedestal mounted, remotely-controlled mechanisms but in one configuration the two columns of three barrels are parallel whereas in the other the top two barrels are closer together than the other two pairs. The former fires all its rockets simultaneously and is thought to be designated RBU-4500, while the second RBU-4500A fires its rounds sequentially.

The range of the rockets used with these launchers has been reported as 2,500 m.

Status
Operational in the Soviet Navy.

6-barrel 300 mm AS rocket launcher.

(USSR)

250 mm ANTI-SUBMARINE ROCKET LAUNCHERS

Three different types of mounting for 250 mm calibre anti-submarine rockets have been observed; and it is believed that the performance of rockets launched from one of these — the earliest in service — is inferior to that of rockets launched from the other two.

This "inferior" model is the five-barrel RBU-1800 launcher. The range of these rockets is said to be some 1,800 m: launch tube length is 180 cm — as also is that of the other two launchers.

The more recent models are the 12-barrel RBU-2500 and 16-barrel RBU-2500A launchers. Range of rockets launched is said to be about 2,500 m for the former, and 6,000 m for the latter launchers. Part of the performance of RBU-2500A projectiles may be due to the suspected use of a gas-injection system to boost them from the launcher tubes.

Status

Weapons of these three types are very extensively deployed in the Soviet Navy. The 1,800 m launchers are mainly deployed on small craft of Warsaw Pact naval forces.

5-barrelled RBU-1800 anti-submarine rocket launchers aboard Soviet fast-attack craft.

2 × 12 barrelled 250 mm anti-submarine rocket launchers aboard *Krivak* class destroyer.

DEPTH CHARGES AND LAUNCHERS

Since the introduction of the anti-submarine depth charge by the Royal Navy in 1916 many devices have been used to create a pattern of underwater explosions having a reasonable chance of critically damaging a submarine.

Fixed Launchers

The modern equivalents of the original simple cylindrical depth charge and their fixed launchers are still widely deployed; and although in some quarters this type of anti-submarine warfare is regarded as obsolescent — because the depth charges must be launched from a moving ship and because the necessarily long interval between launch and explosion (to enable the launching ship to get clear) increases the submarine's chances of escape — they are likely to remain in service for some years yet.

Fixed launching arrangements for depth charges of this sort consist of simple rails, from which the charges are dropped into the sea, and fixed spigot mortars, catapults or similar devices, operated by small explosive charges or compressed air, whereby the charge can be projected 100 m or more from the ship. A combination of rails and launchers with suitable timing can produce a pattern of explosions of pre-determined shape and dimensions.

Trainable Launchers

Beginning in the Second World War and continuing to the present day there have been sporadic outbursts of development activity resulting in a variety of ASW mortars whose direction and angle of fire can be controlled and which fire a streamlined depth charge with a higher sinking rate to a greater distance from a ship which need not be in motion. Currently operational weapons of this type are described individually in the entries that follow, which deal with weapons developed or manufactured in Australia, Britain, France, Italy and Sweden. So far as is known, no weapon of this type has been developed in the USSR: both there and in the USA the preference, in longer-range anti-submarine weapon technology, has been for rocket-propelled charges.

Typical Characteristics
Calibre: 305 mm (12-inch)
Weight: 150 kg
Explosive: 134 kg
Fuze: hydrostatic
Depth limit: down to approx 90 m (50 fathoms)
Maximum projected range: 160 m
Date introduced: 1940 for these characteristics

Status
Operational in various forms throughout the world.

MODIFIED LIMBO ANTI-SUBMARINE MORTAR

(AUSTRALIA)

An improved version of the AS Mk 10 (Limbo) system has been developed in Australia. The new development eliminates the use of rotating electric machinery in the pitch and roll servo loops — with consequent saving in power, deck-level weight and noise — reduces the weight and noise level of the loading mechanisms (pneumatic for Limbo) and eliminates the mechanical problems that can arise from the use of uniselectors in the fuze-setting system.

In the new design the metadyne servo-control system for pitch and roll has been replaced by an electric system using silicon-controlled rectifiers to control the launcher drive motors; the pneumatic rammer has been replaced by a smaller and lighter electrical device; and the fuze-setting system has been redesigned to use solid-stage logic circuits with which have been incorporated additional supervisory circuits that permit checking of the setting before launch.

One effect of all these changes — apart from reduction in cost, weight and noise — is a manning reduction from seven to three.

Manufacturer
Sponsoring Organisation: Department of Manufacturing Industry — Weapons Research Establishment

Status
Production equipments are being delivered to the Royal Australian Navy.

(UK)

Limbo is the successor to the Squid anti-submarine mortar and was developed during the 1950s — also at the Admiralty Underwater Weapons Establishment. Designated AS Mk 10 it is currently the standard anti-submarine mortar of the Royal Navy and several others (reference should be made also, however, to the Australian modification of the system).

The principle of operation is the same as that of the earlier system but Limbo is a more highly mechanical device and thus more flexible operationally. The mortar is stabilised in pitch and roll, loading is pneumatic and the fuzes are set by remote control. The weapon also has a longer range than the Squid.

LIMBO ANTI-SUBMARINE MORTAR

Weapon Data
Calibre: 305 mm (12-inch)
Projectile weight: 200 kg
Range: 1,000-2,000 m
Date introduced: 1955

Status
In widespread operational use.

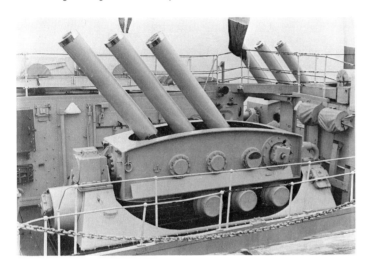

Limbo anti-submarine mortar.

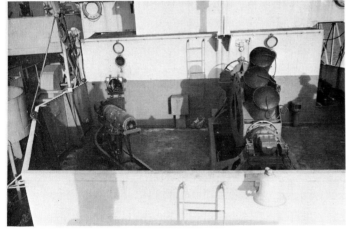

Squid anti-submarine mortar.

(UK)

This was the first of the trainable anti-submarine depth-charge mortars. It was developed by the British Admiralty Underwater Weapon Establishment during the 1940s and is still in service in older ships of many navies.

Position data from the ship's sonar are used by a predictor to compute the mortar aiming position. The three-barrel mortar then fires its depth charges which are programmed to give a three-dimensional explosion pattern ahead of the target. The charges can be set to explode at variable depths using hydrostatic and delayed-action fuzes.

SQUID ANTI-SUBMARINE MORTAR

Weapon Data
Calibre: 305 mm (12-inch)
Projectile weight: 200 kg
Range: approx 400 m
Date introduced: about 1948

Status
Obsolescent but still in widespread use. The obsolescence stems primarily from its lack of operational flexibility compared with later devices.

MENON ANTI-SUBMARINE MORTAR

(ITALY)

This is the earlier of two Italian anti-submarine mortar systems and is currently in service in various destroyers and frigates of the Italian Navy.

It is a turret-mounted device which is generally mounted so that it has an arc of fire extending something like 150° on either side of the forward direction. The mortar is programmed by an anti-submarine weapon control system which in turn derives its information from sonar and own ship data.

Weapon Data
Calibre: 305 mm
Projectile weight: 160 kg
Range: 1,500 m
Date introduced: 1956

Status
Operational but no longer in production.

FOUR-BARREL ANTI-SUBMARINE MORTAR

(FRANCE/SWEDEN)

This system was developed by Bofors in Sweden, subsequently taken up by their licensees, CAFL, and is now regarded as more a French than a Swedish system.

Unlike other AS mortar systems, this one is also intended for use as a shore bombardment mortar, firing a smaller bomb over a longer range. In its anti-submarine role it functions, like other modern mortar systems, in conjunction with a sonar-plus-computer system; and like the Italian system it is turret-mounted with a good forward field of fire and is automatically loaded. As can be seen from the following data, it has the longest range and the heaviest projectile of all current AS mortar systems.

Weapon Data
Calibre: 305 mm
Projectile weight: 230 kg anti-submarine, 100 kg bombardment
Range: 400-2,750 m anti-submarine, 6,000 m bombardment
Date introduced: 1959

Status
Operational in the destroyer *Aconit* and some frigates of the French Navy and on a small scale elsewhere.

SINGLE-BARREL ANTI-SUBMARINE MORTAR

(ITALY)

More recently introduced than the three-barrelled Menon mortar, these Whitehead weapons equip the more modern frigates of the Italian Navy. They are noted for their high rate of fire.

Like the three-barrelled weapon, they are turret-mounted with a good forward field of fire. Fire control is by an Elsag DLB-1 FCS.

There are believed to be two models of this mortar, designated K112 and K113: the following data are believed to relate to the K113.

Weapon Data
Calibre: 305 mm
Projectile weight: 160 kg
Range: approx 1,000 m
Rate of fire: 15 rounds/min
Date introduced: 1960

Manufacturer
Whitehead Moto Fides

Status
In service as stated.

HEDGEHOG ANTI-SUBMARINE SPIGOT MORTARS

(USA)

"Hedgehog" is a name given generally to a family of multiple ahead-throwing spigot mortars designed to produce a patterned fall of shot in an area believed to contain a submarine. The projectiles are small bombs with a high sinking rate and contact fuzes and are intended to disable the submarine by striking it — one or two bombs being sufficient to do this.

The system was originally developed in the USA during the Second World War and has since been taken up by many other countries. The original design was a fixed system giving a single oval pattern of 24 bombs directly ahead of the launcher, and fixed launchers of subsequent marks are widely deployed today. In the meantime, however, more elaborate trainable launchers associated with more sophisticated fire-control systems have been developed.

Weapon Data
Calibre: 127 mm (5-inch)
Projectile weight: 26 kg
Range: 350 m
Date introduced: 1943 onwards

Status
In widespread use in many different versions.

The term "Hedgehog" should strictly be confined to 24-bomb launchers: a smaller device using only eight bombs is known as "Mousetrap". The term is, however, often misapplied to a variety of multiple bomb launching devices.

(USA)

MOUSETRAP ANTI-SUBMARINE SPIGOT MORTARS

"Mousetrap" was the name given to a multiple spigot mortar weapon similar in principle to, but smaller than, the Hedgehog. It used the same bomb as Hedgehog but had a shorter range and fired a pattern of eight instead of 24 bombs.

Weapon Data
Calibre: 127 mm (5-inch)
Projectile weight: 26 kg
Range: approx 200 m
Date introduced: 1944

Status
Various marks of this weapon and similar weapons are to be found in many navies.

Hedgehog anti-submarine spigot mortars, Second World War-vintage.

LATEST DEVELOPMENTS

STAND-OFF WEAPON   (USA)

Intended to replace the SUBROC and ASROC weapons, this new missile is being developed by Boeing and Gould. It is expected to have a range of 90 km and to be effective against the latest types of deep-diving submarines. Alternative nuclear and conventional payloads will be developed.

SUBMARINE-LAUNCHED MOBILE MINE   (USA)

Little is known about this shallow-water bottom mine, except that it uses what the US Department of Defense terms "a converted torpedo". Procurement is due to begin in Fiscal Year 1982.

5 inch GUIDED PROJECTILE   (USA)

In order to increase the accuracy of its Mk 42 and Mk 45 gun mountings, the US Navy is developing a 5 inch calibre guided projectile. This semi-active laser-homing weapon will have a greater range than the current unguided projectiles and will be compatible with the US Navy's Seafire laser rangefinder.

Missile Data
Length: 154 cm
Launch weight: 47 kg
Propulsion: none (gun launched)
Guidance: semi-active laser homing

Manufacturer
Martin-Marietta (Orlando division)

Status
Under development.

SELF-INITIATING ANTI-AIRCRAFT MISSILE   (USA)

As its title suggests, the Self-Initiating Anti-Aircraft Missile (SIAM) requires no target designation, tracking or illumination facilities. Guidance is by means of a dual mode active-radar/passive infra-red seeker. After being vertically launched by a rocket booster, the round carries out a radar search of the entire hemisphere, detecting and locking on to its target. The missile then turns to align itself with the target before the main rocket motor is lit. Final interception is by infra-red homing.

SIAM is intended to protect surface ships, submarines and high-value point targets. Several test rounds have been fired from the White Sands missile range, the first fully-guided interception of a QH-50 drone helicopter taking place in April 1980.

Missile Data
Length: about 250 cm
Diameter: 32 cm
Launch weight: 68 kg
Propulsion: solid-propellant rocket
Guidance: active radar plus infra-red terminal homing

Manufacturer
Ford Aerospace

Status
Under development.

(JAPAN)

This turbojet-powered missile is being developed from the rocket-powered ASM-1 air-launch weapon. Intended for surface launch, it has about twice the range of the original version. First flight was expected during 1981.

XSSM-2

Missile Data
Length: around 400 cm
Diameter: 35 cm
Launch weight: around 600 kg?
Propulsion: turbofan?
Guidance: intertial plus active-radar seeker
Warhead: 200 kg high-explosive?
Range: at least 50 km

Manufacturer
Mitsubishi

Status
Under development.

(FRANCE)

A submarine-launched version of Exocet is being developed to arm French Navy submarines. Like the US Harpoon, this version will be encapsulated in a container and launched from the submarine's torpedo tubes.

EXOCET SM39

(ISRAEL)

This semi-active homing missile is intended to protect all classes of warship against aircraft or missile attack. The 2.5-tonne eight-round launcher is based on the company's TCM-30 gun mounting and also carries a dual-frequency monopulse target tracking and illumination radar. No details of performance have been released, but the weapon is around 250 cm long and probably weighs 100 kg or more. Maximum range could be 10 km or more.

BARAK

(INTERNATIONAL)

An international team of companies including Contraves (radar tracker), Elettronica (electronic-warfare equipment), Oerlikon (Sea Zenith gun), Plessey (Dolphin search radar) and Siemens (electro-optical sensors) are collaborating on this point-defence system. Both the gun and tracking radar and sensors are fitted with mounts offering coverage of the zenith, in order to counter high-angle diving targets. Firing trials of the Sea Zenith 25 mm gun began in May 1981.

SEA GUARD

INDEX